QUICK-FIX
HOME REPAIR
HANDBOOK

QUICK-FIX
HOME REPAIR
HANDBOOK

KATIE AND GENE HAMILTON

ILLUSTRATIONS BY RAY SKIBINSKI

Galahad Books · New York

First Galahad Books edition published in 1995.

Galahad Books
A division of Budget Book Service, Inc.
386 Park Avenue South
New York, NY 10016

Galahad Books is a registered trademark of Budget Book Service, Inc.

Published by arrangement with GuildAmerica Books, a division of
Doubleday Book & Music Clubs, Inc.

Library of Congress Catalog Card Number: 95-75109

ISBN: 0-88365-897-6

Printed in the United States of America.

Contents

Introduction

Your home is like a giant appliance filled with intricate, intriguing, and often exasperating parts. Yet even though it is your greatest investment, a house doesn't come with an instruction manual. This book is the manual you never received. We hope it helps you understand how things work in your home and what to do when they don't.

Our feeling is that there are two kinds of information about a house: need-to-know and nice-to-know. This book is strictly need-to-know facts about basic home repairs.

Nothing is easy to do for the first time, and home repairs are no exception. We'll take you through the step-by-steps of each repair to familiarize you with each project.

Most other do-it-yourself books imply that anyone can make repairs, but we take a more realistic approach. Some of you don't have the time. Some of you don't want to invest in the tools required. And let's face it, some of you don't have the skill or the temperament. That's okay. We keep this in mind and explain everything that's involved in a repair so you can make the decision to tackle it yourself or hire someone to do it.

This book is for armchair reading to give you an overview of a project. Even if you have no intention of making a repair yourself, you need to know the language. Example: A contractor explains that in order to repair your gutters your fascia board needs to be replaced. Well, we think you should know what fascia board is before giving him the go-ahead.

But don't worry, we are not going to load you down with a vocabulary you don't need to learn. Our aim is to discuss basic home repairs simply and concisely and supplement each repair with clear, simplified line drawings.

We want you to be less intimidated the next time you peruse the aisles of a hardware store or home center, where often the vast array of replacement parts and repair products can be staggering. Make a few exploratory visits to hardware stores and home centers in your neighborhood. Look for a store where you feel comfortable. Choose a store with hours convenient to your schedule. Do they deliver large orders for free? Will they loan or rent tools? Do they offer instruction seminars?

Ask questions of the personnel. Some large chain stores place "Help" telephones throughout the aisles so customers can pick up a phone if they need assistance. Other stores rely on customers who return because of the knowledgeable on-floor sales force. Find out if the store is service-oriented or if you're on your own. Where you prefer shopping is a question only you can answer.

When it is possible, shop for home repair supplies on your own. There is a lot to see and learn from the product display racks and it's unfair to ask children or even other friends or family, who may become impatient, to accompany you.

Don't go empty-handed into the hardware store; take along a compact notebook in which you list the repairs you'll be making and what materials you need to buy for them. If you're looking for a replacement part, bring the old one with you. When that's not possible, note the number or any markings on the part in your notebook. Also use this notebook to keep price records for comparative shopping and to record your home's room dimensions for quick reference.

And now, about tools—let's start off with a section that will explain how they're used and show what they look like.

Tools

In this section you'll find a list of tools that are helpful in making basic household repairs. It's important to keep all tools in one easily accessible place and always put them back when you're through using them. A large plastic crate makes an inexpensive storage bin, and a small tool or fishing tackle box is convenient for storing small items like nails, brads, drill bits, and a measuring tape.

You don't need to go out and buy these tools all at once; and you don't need to own all of them. That's why we specify the suggested tools for each specific project. Most likely, with each project you tackle, you'll add a tool to your inventory, spreading the investment out over a period of time. Buy the highest-quality tool that you can afford.

We like the new cordless power tools because new developments in battery technology have made them lightweight and easy to handle, yet powerful enough for heavy-duty work. Don't be intimidated. Operating a cordless drill is just like using a hair dryer or hand-held blender. The new cordless tools are quieter, too.

One last word, before you start in with any of the repairs, read the instructions through carefully. This way you can better determine the relative ease or difficulty of the specific repair and whether all or only certain tools specified may be necessary to complete the job.

BASIC TOOLS:

Closet auger: crank-handled device used for unclogging a toilet.

Trap and drain auger: twisted metal snakelike device that you direct to force an opening in a blocked plumbing line.

Wire brush: tool for cleaning rust from metal and preparing wood and masonry surfaces for painting.

Carpenters level: tool that determines whether a surface is level or vertical; useful for installing drapery rods, pictures, shelving, etc.

Caulking gun: metal or plastic pistol-like holder that dispenses caulk or adhesive from a cartridge.

Cold chisel: strong steel tool often used with a hammer to chip away heavy material like mortar or brickwork.

C-clamp: adjustable device that holds surfaces together while you work on them or during assembly to allow glue to set.

Hand drill: crank-operated tool that works much like an eggbeater; used for installing screws into walls, wood, and metal; the type of bit (the part of the drill that makes the hole) is determined by the kind of surface you're drilling into.

⅜″ Power drill: essential tool because of its wide range of attachments, i.e., buffing pad, sanding disk; with the correct bit you can make holes in a wide variety of surfaces; electric or cordless.

Fuse puller: insulated tongs used to remove cartridge fuses.

Claw hammer: kind of hammer used to insert and pull out nails in wood or wall surfaces.

Putty knife: metal bladed knife about 2 inches wide, used to spread wood filler or Spackle compound into holes and cracks.

Utility knife: one of the most often used tools around the house, i.e., cutting floor tile, trimming wallpaper, scoring lines, and opening heavy cardboard packages; the handle often comes apart in two halves and provides a storage place for extra blades.

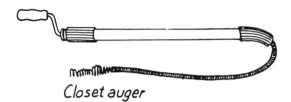
Closet auger

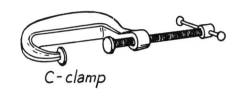
C-clamp

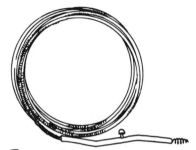
Trap and drain auger

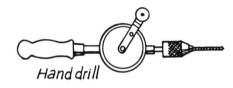
Hand drill

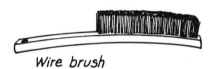
Wire brush

3/8" Power drill

Carpenters level

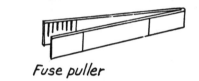
Fuse puller

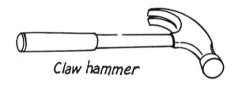
Claw hammer

Caulking gun

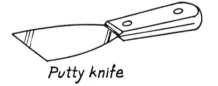
Putty knife

Cold chisel

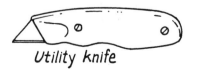
Utility knife

3

Steel measuring tape: flexible tape marked in inches and feet, used for marking and measuring; thumb-lock feature to keep tape from rewinding is an added plus.

Multipurpose electrical tool: pliers-like tool that cuts wire and strips the insulation off without nicking the wire.

Nail set: pointed steel shaft used with a hammer to drive nails below the surface.

Plane: hand-held cutting tool used for smoothing a wood surface and making it flat, or to reduce the height, width or thickness of a door, etc.

Pliers: tool used to cut and shape wires and to grip something firmly; different types are distinguished by their "nose" (needle nose, etc.); a channel-lock pliers has a multiple-channel slip joint between its jaws to allow a much wider range of adjustment than a standard pliers.

"Plumber's helper" plunger: rubber suction cup on a wooden stick used to force out clogs in plumbing lines, i.e., toilet, sink, tub.

Crosscut saw: handy tool for general cutting purposes, like on paneling and lumber; usually two feet long with eight to ten teeth per inch.

General purpose scissors: suitable tool for cutting fabric or wallpaper.

Paint scraper: metal blade, about 2 inches wide, on a sturdy handle, used to remove loose dried paint.

Cordless power screwdriver: lightweight tool designed to replace a standard screwdriver; comes with a variety of interchangeable screwheads.

Phillips screwdriver: crosshead screwdriver for screws with two intersecting slots; comes in various sizes.

Standard-blade or single-slot screwdriver: tool used to insert screws into various surfaces; comes in various sizes.

Try square: useful tool to test for squareness of adjoining surfaces, such as during window screen repair.

Adjustable wrench: tool used to loosen and tighten nuts and bolts; also used in plumbing jobs like fitting faucets.

Nail set

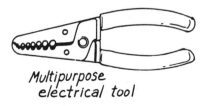
Steel measuring tape

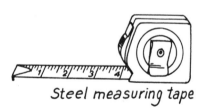
Multipurpose electrical tool

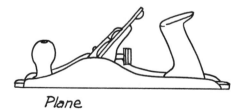
Plane

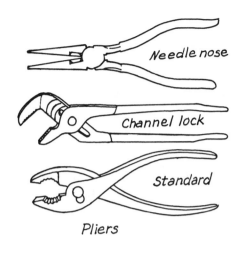

Needle nose

Channel lock

Standard

Pliers

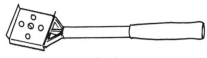

Paint scraper

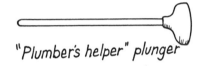

"Plumber's helper" plunger

Cordless power screwdriver

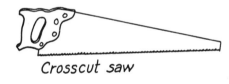

Crosscut saw

Phillips screwdriver

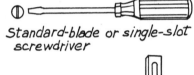

Standard-blade or single-slot screwdriver

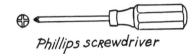

Try square

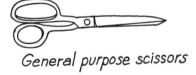

General purpose scissors

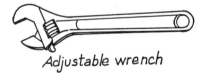

Adjustable wrench

Safety Guidelines

Here are some suggestions to help ensure a safe environment for making home repairs:

• ALWAYS wear a pair of inexpensive plastic safety goggles for eye protection when using tools that strike or chip, i.e., removing old putty from a window sash, hammering nails.

• Remove any jewelry; roll up your shirt sleeves; if you have long hair, pull it back.

• When wallpapering, always turn OFF the electricity in the room. Otherwise, you run the risk of touching a live wire near an outlet that will shock you.

• When painting or refinishing a surface, make sure the area is well lighted and well ventilated.

• When using a ladder, make sure that it is on solid, nonslippery footing, with the ladder's base one fourth the ladder's height away from the wall or building. Don't lean over to reach the work area; stay close to the ladder's rails. Move your ladder closer to the work area, if necessary. Don't stand on the top step or rung of any ladder.

• Before removing a broken light bulb, turn off the electricity that serves the fixture.

• When working on an electrical appliance, do not open the appliance or work on it until the cord is unplugged from the power source.

• Keep electrical cords out of the way when not in use and make sure they are properly grounded.

• Store tools so they cannot fall and become damaged, or damage others. Cover sharp-edged tools so you don't hurt yourself rummaging around a drawer to find one.

• Keep your tools clean and your edged tools sharpened; a dull tool doesn't work properly and can slip from your grip.

• Store paint thinners and solvents in their original cans or in safety containers.

• Place oily rags in airtight cans and dispose of them promptly.

• Keep a fire extinguisher handy.

• Keep all tools, solvents, and chemicals out of the reach of small children.

SECTION 1

Plumbing Repairs

Flooding and Other Emergencies

Tools: Adjustable wrench, channel-lock pliers

The motto "Be Prepared" applies to many things in life and one of them is knowing what to do if your kitchen or bathroom is suddenly deluged with water. The following preventive measures will find you prepared in case such an emergency ever occurs.

1) Find and tag the main water valve

Your house or apartment has one central valve, called the *main shut-off valve,* that controls the inflow of all water. You'll find it in the basement or utility area near the water meter or at the floor where the main water line comes into the house or apartment building.

For emergencies, it's helpful if the main shut-off valve has a tag with arrows pointing "on" and "off" directions. Turn the valve clockwise ("off") to close it and counter-clockwise ("on") to open it. Make sure you can open and close the water valve; it may become stuck if it has not been operated for a long time. A channel-lock pliers or adjustable wrench can be used to turn the handle if it's stuck, but don't apply too much force or you could break the valve. If the valve still won't close, seek professional help since it might have to be replaced.

2) Find sink, toilet, and appliance stop valves

All newer and most older homes have individual valves at each fixture called *stop valves* that control the water supply to that individual fixture. Look under the sink or dishwasher, in the bathroom under the vanity or toilet, in the laundry or utility room under the clothes washer or hot water heater. Label each valve with a tag noting which direction to turn it in order to shut off the water flow (usually clockwise). If you don't find a stop valve at each fixture, then the main shut-off valve will have to be turned off in order to stop a leak at the fixture.

When a leak occurs, go to its source and turn off the valve. For example, if you have a leaky faucet, or over-flowing clothes washer, dishwasher or toilet, turn its stop valve off and the water will remain on in the rest of the house.

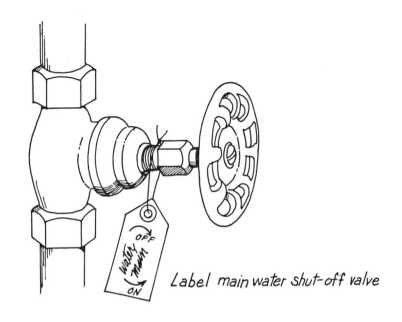

Label main water shut-off valve

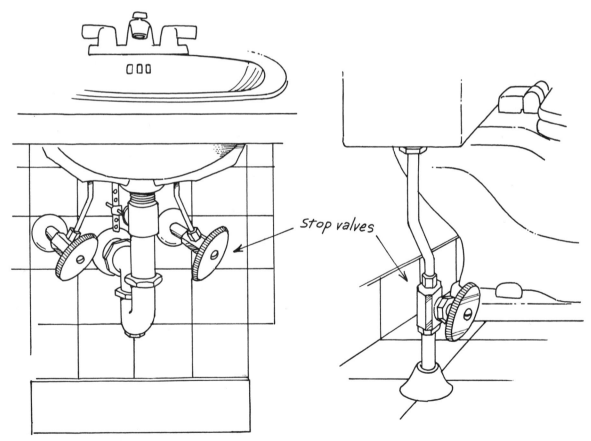

Stop valves

9

Fix a Two-Handle Washer Faucet

Tools: Screwdriver, adjustable wrench or channel-lock pliers

Most older two-handle faucets have a rubber washer that is compressed against a valve seat in the base of the faucet to stop the water flow. After a while the washer wears out and allows water to pass between it and the valve seat. Fixing such a leak is easy. First of all, turn the water off at the stop valve below the fixture or at the main shut-off valve of your home or apartment (see pages 8–9).

1) Remove screw cover, handle screw, and handle

There may be a decorative cover (escutcheon) in the center of the handle which hides the handle screw. If so, use a screwdriver to pry off this cover. Then remove the screw and handle. (*Illustration A.*)

2) Remove packing nut and valve stem

Use an adjustable wrench or channel-lock pliers to remove, by turning counterclockwise, the large packing nut at the top of the faucet body. (*Illustration B.*) Then twist out, counterclockwise, the valve stem. If it is stuck, put the handle back on to give you a better grip on the stem.

3) Replace washer

Look at the end of the stem that fits into the faucet. You should see a brass screw holding the old washer in place. (*Illustration C.*) If there is no screw, just a rubber washer, then you probably have a diaphragm faucet (see pages 12–13). Remove the screw and old washer. The washer is either flat or beveled but sometimes this is difficult to tell since as they wear out, both types become squashed out of shape. If you can't tell what type of washer you need, look into the top of the faucet; the first opening you see is the valve seat. If the lip is angled you need a *beveled washer;* otherwise, a *flat washer.*

Take the stem and old washer to a hardware store or home center and buy replacement washers. They are sold in kits that contain a variety of sizes and extra stem screws. Replace the washer and brass stem screw, then rub some petroleum jelly or light grease on the stem threads and thread the stem into the faucet body. Replace the packing nut and handle. Turn on the faucet. If the water still leaks, the valve seat needs to be refaced or ground smooth. This is not difficult but you need a special tool, so consult a plumbing manual or seek professional help.

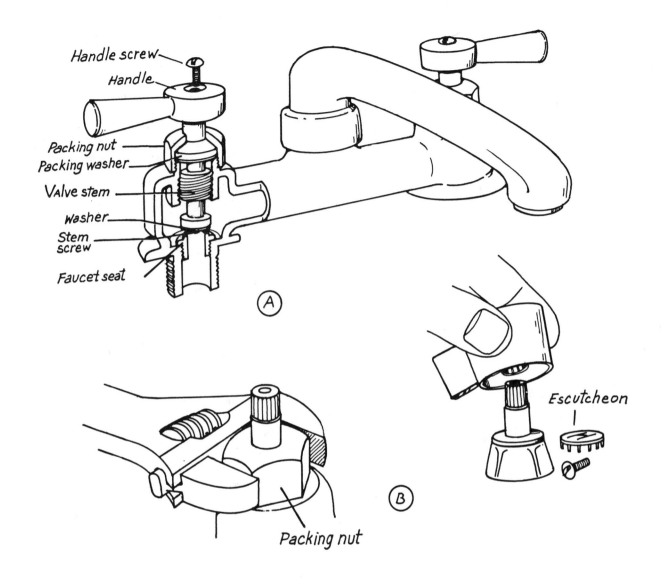

Handle screw

Handle

Packing nut

Packing washer

Valve stem

Washer

Stem screw

Faucet seat

(A)

Packing nut

(B)

Escutcheon

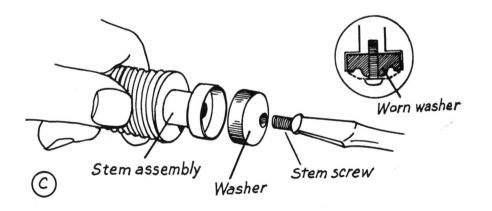

Worn washer

Stem assembly

Washer

Stem screw

(C)

11

Fix a Two-Handle Diaphragm Faucet

Tools: Screwdriver, adjustable wrench or channel-lock pliers

Some newer two-handle faucets have a rubber washer that looks like a diaphragm. It is not held in place by a screw (like the faucet shown on page 11) but slips over the end of the stem. Like standard washers, after a while the washer wears out and allows water to seep between it and the valve seat in the faucet base. If this occurs, turn the water off at the stop valve below the fixture or at the main shut-off valve of your home or apartment (see pages 8–9).

1) Remove screw cover, handle screw, and handle

There is usually a decorative cover (escutcheon) in the center of the handle which hides the handle screw. If so, use a screwdriver to pry this cover off. Then remove the screw and handle.

2) Remove packing nut and stem

Use an adjustable wrench or a channel-lock pliers to remove, by turning counterclockwise, the locknut at the top of the faucet body. (*Illustration A.*) Then twist out, counterclockwise, the valve stem. If it is stuck, put the handle back on to give you a better grip on the stem.

3) Replace diaphragm

Look at the end of the stem (the stem tip) that fits into the faucet. If no screw is visible, take the stem and rubber washer to your local hardware store or home center and purchase a replacement diaphragm. If you see a brass screw projecting out of the washer, identify the kind of washer you'll need to replace (see Step 3, page 10).

Replace the diaphragm by slipping it over the stem tip. (*Illustration B.*) Check that there is no dirt or particles between the rubber and the end of the stem. Rub some petroleum jelly or light grease on the stem threads and screw the stem into the faucet body. Replace the locknut. (*Illustration C.*) Then replace the handle. Turn on the faucet. If the water still leaks, the valve seat (see illustration, page 11) needs to be refaced or ground smooth. This is not difficult but you need a special tool, so consult a plumbing manual or seek professional help.

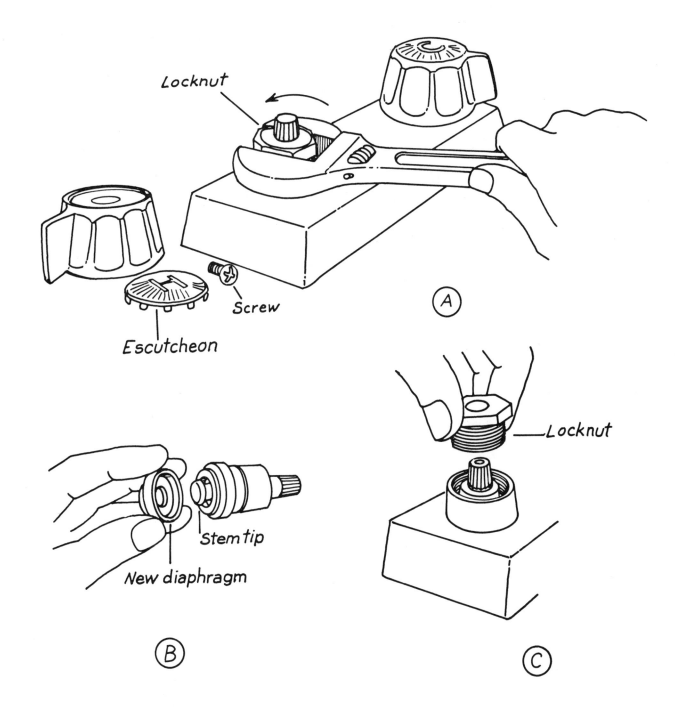

Locknut

Screw

Escutcheon

(A)

New diaphragm

Stem tip

(B)

Locknut

(C)

13

Fix a Two-Handle Washerless Faucet

Tools: Screwdriver, adjustable wrench or channel-lock pliers

A disc-type faucet is less likely to need service because the valve does not compress a rubber washer (which eventually deteriorates) to stop the water. When it does need repair, however, you usually replace the whole valve assembly. To tell what type of valve it is, you'll have to take the valve apart. First, turn off the water at the stop valve below the fixture or at the main shut-off valve of your home or apartment (see pages 8–9).

1) Remove screw cover, handle screw, and handle

There is usually a decorative cover (escutcheon) in the center of the handle which hides the handle screw. Use a screwdriver to pry off this cover. Then remove the screw by turning it counterclockwise and pulling the handle up and off the stem.

2) Remove stem nut

Use an adjustable wrench or channel-lock pliers to remove the stem nut by turning it counterclockwise. (*Illustration A.*) If the nut is too large for your wrench, wrap masking tape around the nut to protect its finish and use a channel-lock pliers to loosen the nut.

3) Pull out valve body and replace it

Pull up and out on the valve stem to lift out the valve body. (*Illustration B.*) If it is difficult to remove, replace the handle so you can get a better grip on the stem. At the end of the valve assembly you will see a couple of brass discs or a rubber diaphragm. If, after you remove the valve assembly, you see a bare shaft without a washer on its end, you probably have a disc-type faucet. Take the valve body to your hardware store or home center and buy a complete replacement valve body.

Most replacement parts come with directions and assembly instructions. Follow these tips; or you can reverse the steps you took to remove the valve body, in order to reassemble the faucet.

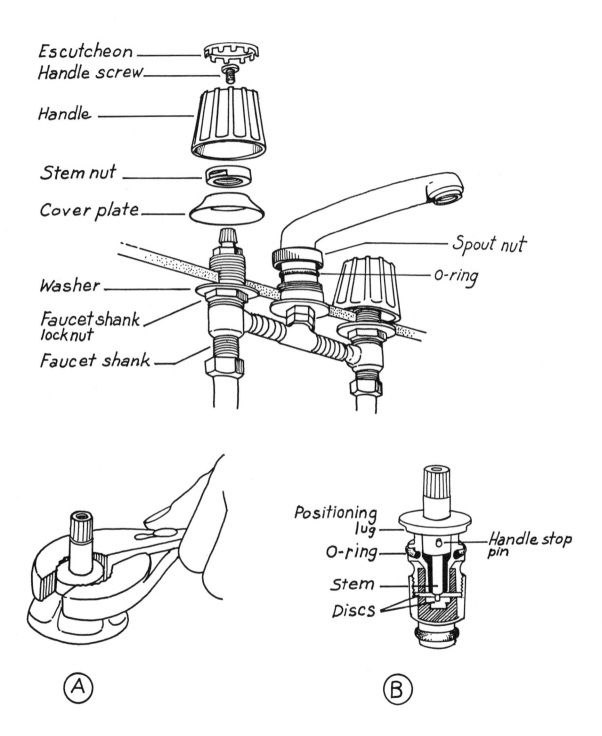

Escutcheon

Handle screw

Handle

Stem nut

Cover plate

Spout nut

O-ring

Washer

Faucet shank lock nut

Faucet shank

Positioning lug

O-ring

Handle stop pin

Stem

Discs

Ⓐ

Ⓑ

15

Fix a Spray Hose or Faucet Aerator

Tools: Channel-lock pliers

Slow water flow at your kitchen sink can usually be traced to a clogged aerator or spray hose nozzle. The aerator is screwed to the end of the sink spout and mixes air into the faucet's water, thus preventing the water from splashing. Both the aerator and the nozzle of the spray hose attachment have small holes that are easily clogged with dirt particles or mineral deposits from the water.

1) Remove and clean aerator parts

The facing illustration shows the main parts of the faucet aerator and spray hose assembly. The aerator is removed by unscrewing it from the end of the spout. If it is tight, wrap masking tape around the aerator and remove it with a channel-lock pliers. Note the order of the aerator parts you remove so you can correctly reassemble them.

Remove the aerator and turn on the water. If the flow is strong, the trouble is a clogged aerator. Clean the aerator disc and screen by pushing a pin or thin wire through the small holes. If the disc and screen are badly clogged or corroded, purchase a new aerator assembly at your local hardware store or home center.

2) Check spray nozzle

If you note a decrease in water flow at the spout of the spray nozzle when you squeeze the spray handle, then you might have a clogged spray head. To clean it, turn the sink faucet off, then loosen the nozzle with a pliers, being careful not to mar the plastic. Next, check the water flow. Turn the water on and squeeze the spray handle again. If a steady flow of water comes out, clean the nozzle and replace it.

3) Check diverter valve

A weak water flow from the spray hose can also be caused by a kinked hose or faulty diverter valve. First, check the hose for any kinks or tangles. Then turn the faucet on and squeeze the handle on the spray head. Most, if not all, of the water should stop coming out of the sink and squirt out the spray head. If the water keeps running out of the sink spout with the same force as it had before you squeezed the spray handle, the diverter valve is faulty or you have a clogged spray nozzle.

The diverter valve is located in the sink faucet. Wrap masking tape around the spout nut and remove it with a channel-lock pliers. Pull the sink spout up and out of the faucet body. Look into the faucet body and you will see the diverter valve. Remove this valve—by lifting or screwing it out counterclockwise—and clean it. Then put it back in place and try the spray again. If you still experience trouble, purchase a replacement diverter valve.

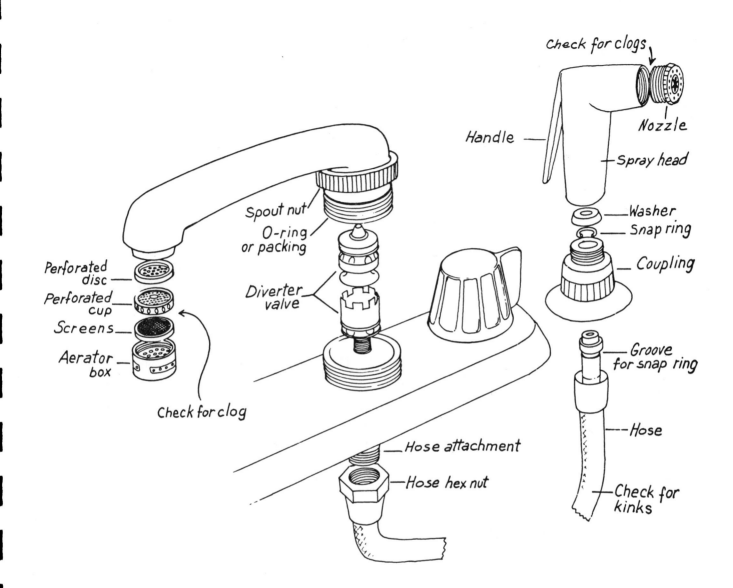

Check for clogs

Handle

Nozzle

Spray head

Spout nut

O-ring or packing

Washer

Snap ring

Coupling

Perforated disc

Perforated cup

Diverter valve

Screens

Aerator box

Groove for snap ring

Check for clog

Hose

Hose attachment

Hose hex nut

Check for kinks

Fix a Leaky Faucet Stem or Spout

Tools: Channel-lock pliers, screwdriver, adjustable wrench

Most older two-handle faucets have packing around the valve stem, just under the packing nut, to stop water from leaking out around the base of the handle. Newer faucets with movable spouts have either packing or an O-ring that in time will wear. A small puddle of water at the base of your kitchen faucet could be caused by leaking packing or worn O-ring.

Replacing the stem packing in older faucets is easy, but sometimes the whole valve assembly has to be replaced on the newer types of faucets with O-rings. The spout packing or O-ring can also be easily replaced. First, turn off the water at the stop valve below the fixture or at the main shut-off valve of your home or apartment (see pages 8–9).

FAUCET SPOUT

1) Tighten spout nut

In many cases leaks from the base of a faucet's spout can be stopped by simply tightening the spout nut with pliers. The spout nut is usually located at the base of the spout or hidden under the handle or chrome faucet cover escutcheon.

2) Replace spout nut, if necessary

If tightening the spout nut does not stop the leak, replace the faucet's packing or O-ring. Put masking tape around the nut or ring to protect its finish; then loosen it with channel-lock pliers. Twist the spout nut and pull it straight up and out of the faucet. Take the spout to your local hardware store or home center and purchase new packing or an exact O-ring replacement.

Put petroleum jelly on the new O-ring for ease in reassembling the spout. If you replaced the packing (see location, page 17), check that the new packing fills the space around the spout and is compressed when you tighten the nut or ring.

FAUCET STEM

1) Remove screw cover, handle screw, and handle

There is usually a decorative cover (escutcheon) in the center of the faucet's handle that hides the handle screw. Use a screwdriver to pry this cover off; then remove the screw and handle. (*Illustration A.*)

2) Remove packing nut and stem

Use an adjustable wrench to remove the large packing nut at the top of the faucet body by turning it counterclockwise. Then twist out, counterclockwise, the valve stem. If it is stuck, put the handle back on to give you a better grip on the stem.

Since there are several types of packing and dozens of O-rings at hardware stores and home centers, take the stem and packing nut from your own faucet so you'll be sure to get an exact replacement. (*Illustration B.*) The packing will most likely look like string. (*Illustration C.*)

3) If necessary, make temporary repair to stem

If you can't get to the hardware store, a temporary repair can be made to a faucet that normally has packing by wrapping string around the stem above the old packing. Reassemble the faucet and tighten the packing nut. The string should tighten the old packing enough to temporarily stop the leak. On a newer O-ring-sealed stem, apply petroleum jelly to the O-ring (*Illustration D*) before you reassemble the faucet. It might stop the leak until you can make the permanent repair.

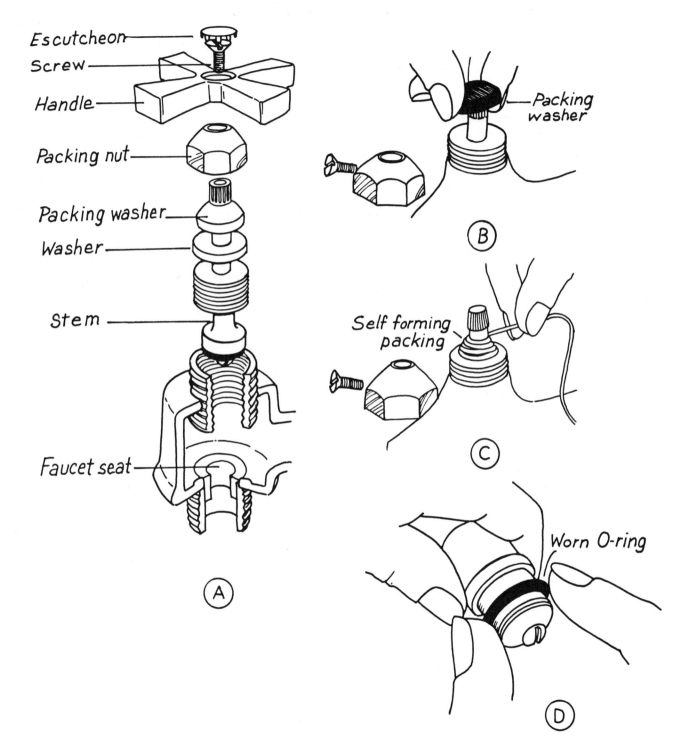

Escutcheon

Screw

Handle

Packing nut

Packing washer

Washer

Stem

Faucet seat

(A)

Packing washer

(B)

Self forming packing

(C)

Worn O-ring

(D)

19

Unclog a Sink Drain

Tools: Plunger, channel-lock pliers, trap and drain auger

Sooner or later you are going to be faced with unclogging a stopped-up drain. The easiest method is to use a liquid drain opener. If this doesn't work, you may have to resort to the trusty "plumber's helper" plunger. For really stubborn clogs you can remove the trap or use an auger.

1) Try a liquid drain opener

When your sink backs up you can try using a chemical drain cleaner, but they are not always effective. Follow the manufacturer's directions carefully. If at all possible, wear protective gloves and plastic safety goggles. These caustic chemicals must be used with caution. Your skin and eyes can be burned from contact with them.

2) Use suction plunger

First, remove the sink strainer or pop-up stopper by pulling it straight up. If it will not come out, make sure it is open as wide as possible. Stuff a rag into the overflow drain of a bathroom sink to increase the plunger suction. If there isn't any standing water in the sink, run a couple of inches of water into it. Put the plunger cup over the drain and push down, then pull up sharply to dislodge the clog. (*Illustration A.*) Work the plunger back and forth several times and you should loosen the clog.

When the standing water runs out of the sink, remove the rag from the overflow opening. Turn on the water and allow it to run for a few minutes to wash the clog completely out of the pipe. Don't allow the water to run unattended. The sink might clog again and overflow.

3) Remove trap

A third alternative, if chemicals or plunging don't clear a drain, is to remove the U-shaped trap below the sink. Place a bucket beneath the trap and loosen the two large nuts at each end of the trap with a channel-lock pliers. Drain the water out of the trap into the bucket (*Illustration B*). Loosen the nut to remove the trap, and clean out the trap with a strong detergent. Also clean the drain opening leading out of the sink. Remove the pop-up assembly, if necessary.

If the trap is clean but the drain is still not clear, then the clog is farther down the pipe. Bend a wire hanger so it will fit into the pipe and push it in as far as you can. Then twist it around and try to snag the obstruction.

4) Use trap and drain auger

If you cannot snag any obstruction in the drain with a coat hanger, then borrow or buy a trap and drain auger. This flexible "snake" can work its way around corners and down the pipe until it reaches the clog. (*Illustration C.*)

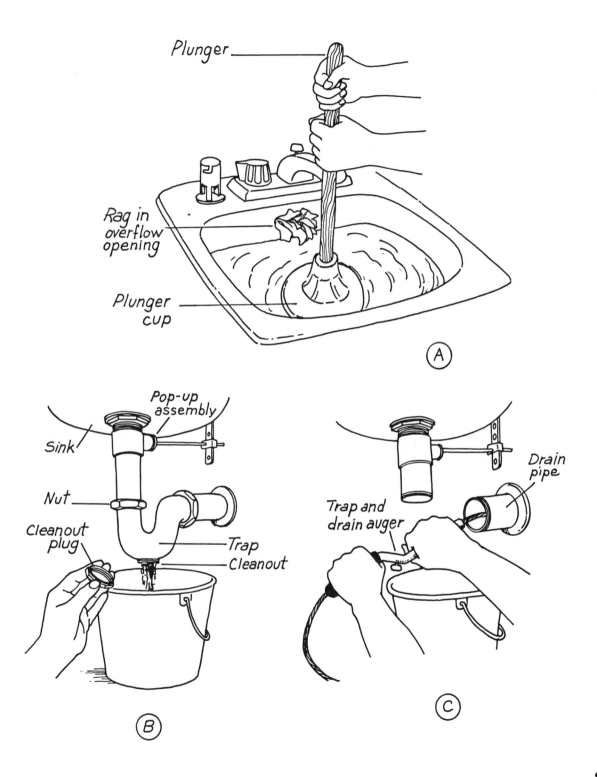

Plunger

Rag in
overflow
opening

Plunger
cup

(A)

Pop-up
assembly

Sink

Nut

Cleanout
plug

Trap

Cleanout

(B)

Drain
pipe

Trap and
drain auger

(C)

21

Unclog a Bathtub Drain

Tools: Plunger, trap and drain auger, channel-lock pliers, adjustable wrench

Many bathtub clogs are caused by hair caught in the pop-up drain linkage or in the drum trap. A wad of hair stuck in a drain is messy but not difficult to free, while a clogged drum trap can be a real challenge to clear.

Begin with the first easy steps described below. If these don't start the water flowing, then move to the next procedure. Eventually you will get the drain open.

1) Remove drain plug and check linkage for hair

If your tub has an X-shaped strainer or a drain that you can open or close from a lever just below the water spout, the clog may be caused by hair caught on the strainer or lifting linkage inside the drain pipe. Another type mechanism has an internal plunger.

Pull up on the drain plug and some of the hair stuck in the drain should come out. Look inside the drain opening and you will probably see a mass of hair wrapped around the rocker arm linkage attached to the drain plug.

Remove as much hair as possible—a coat hanger bent into a hook may be helpful—and pull the drain plug and linkage from the drain. With the drain open, try running the water. If the tub drains freely, clean the drain plug and put it back into position.

2) Try liquid drain opener

If, after removing all hair buildup, you find that the drain is still clogged, try using a chemical drain cleaner. Follow the manufacturer's directions carefully. Wear protective gloves and glasses, if at all possible, and use these caustic chemicals cautiously. Your skin and eyes can be burned from contact with them. Don't allow the drain opener chemical to sit in the tub for a long time since it can damage a porcelain finish.

3) Use plunger to open drain line

Another possibility to open a drain line is to remove the drain plug and most of the hair, then plug the overflow drain with a rag. Fill the tub with a few inches of water and work the plunger up and down, pulling up sharply to dislodge the clog, then working the plunger back and forth several times. (*Illustration A.*) When the standing water begins to run out of the sink, remove the rag from the overflow drain. Then let the water run for a few minutes to wash the clog completely out of the drain line.

4) Use trap and drain auger to snare clog

If a plunger doesn't do the trick, use an auger. Run it through the overflow drain or into the drain directly. Remove the cover on the overflow drain. Insert the auger into the overflow drain and push it down as far as it will go. (*Illustration B.*) Crank the handle slowly in a clockwise direction and keep pushing it farther into the pipe. Eventually you should come to the clog; break it up or snare the end of it with the auger and pull the obstruction out.

5) Clean out drum trap

If your bathtub has a drum trap, a round plate in the floor or a P-trap behind the wall, here's how to unclog it. If you have a drum trap, use an adjustable wrench to remove the plug. The drum trap might be rusted shut, in which case no amount of effort on your part will open it, short of breaking the top cover. If you can't budge the cover and the clog persists, call professional help. If you can get the cover off, run an auger through it back toward the overflow drain of the tub.

If that doesn't work, the blockage is in the main drain and you should call a plumber.

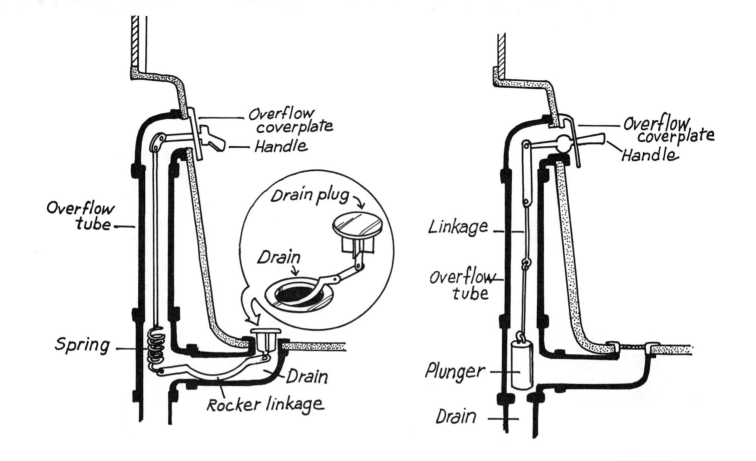

Overflow coverplate

Handle

Overflow tube

Spring

Drain plug

Drain

Drain

Rocker linkage

Overflow coverplate

Handle

Linkage

Overflow tube

Plunger

Drain

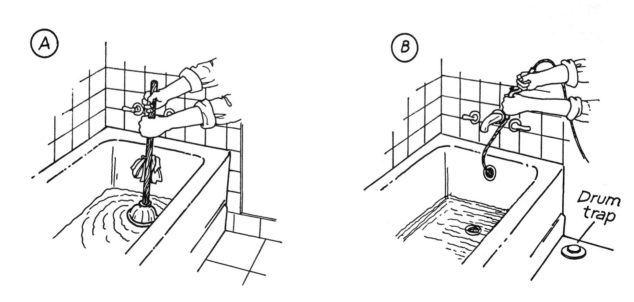

(A)

(B)

Drum trap

Fix a Leaky Toilet

Tools: Screwdriver

Running water in the toilet is an annoying and costly problem. Even a slow leak can waste hundreds of gallons of water a week. The cause of such leaking is usually not difficult to fix.

1) Identify parts of toilet mechanism

All tank-type flush toilets work the same. Remove the top of the tank and set it aside in a secure place; it will break if it falls. Push the toilet's flush lever and look inside. You will see that the flush handle lifts a round rubber tank ball or rubber flapper to let water flow into the toilet bowl. As the tank empties, the large float ball attached to the end of a long rod falls with the water level in the tank. At the other end of the rod is the intake valve (which opens as the float ball moves down) that will feed water into the tank. When the tank is just about empty, the tank ball falls into the outlet, stopping the flow of water to the toilet bowl, and the tank begins to fill from the open inlet valve. You will most likely find the trouble in one of three places: the tank ball, inlet valve, or float ball. Remember: The water in the toilet tank is clean; don't worry about putting your hands in it.

2) Check float ball and inlet valve

If after the tank refills, the water keeps running into the tank and spilling out of the overflow pipe, the trouble is in the float mechanism or in the inlet valve.

The float ball should float in the water and resist any pressure to push it under. Try to push it down. If the float has a leak, it won't pop back up. If this is the case, unscrew it from the rod, turning it counterclockwise, and take it to a hardware store for a replacement.

If the ball is floating and the water in the tank continues to run, lift up on the float ball and the water should stop. If it does, bend the rod down to lower the float ball. (*Illustration A.*) Release the float ball and check for running water. If the water still runs, bend the rod down more until the water stops. Flush the toilet and check for leaking. If after several tries of bending the float rod it does not stop the water, then the problem is in the intake valve. Fixing this valve is not difficult, but since there are so many types of valves, you will be better off seeking professional help.

3) Test trip lever and tank ball

If the tank does not fill or you have to wiggle the flush handle up and down to get the tank ball to fall into the outlet pipe, the trouble is with the tank ball mechanism.

Reach into the tank and pull up on the wire that the tank ball is attached to. This wire and tank ball should slide up and down easily and drop straight down into the outlet pipe. Bend this wire (only slight adjustment is needed), and the one leading up to the arm connected to the flush lever, until the tank ball works freely. Flush the toilet and check how the toilet tank refills.

4) Replace tank ball valve

If after several attempts you cannot get the tank ball to fall into the outlet pipe and stop the water flow, go to the hardware store and buy a flapper-type tank ball. Remove the old tank ball by unscrewing it from the end of the brass rod; then remove the rod. Follow the instructions included in the package for easy installation.

Standard flush mechanism

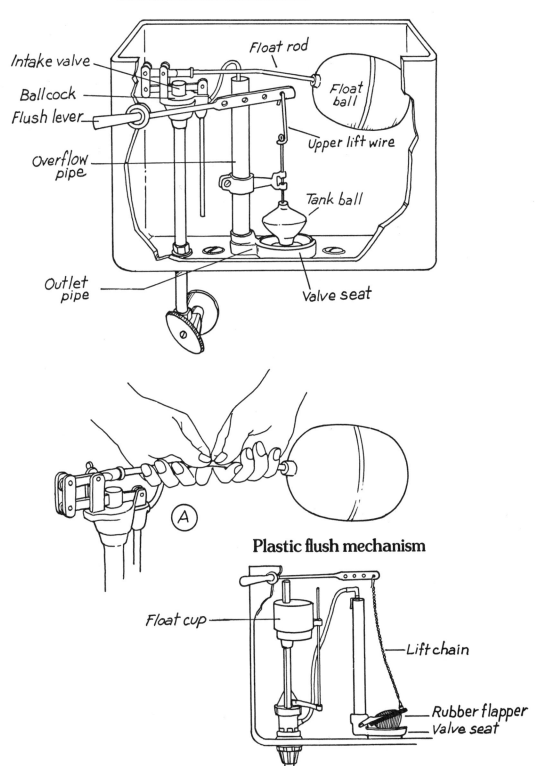

Intake valve

Ballcock

Flush lever

Overflow pipe

Outlet pipe

Float rod

Float ball

Upper lift wire

Tank ball

Valve seat

(A)

Plastic flush mechanism

Float cup

Lift chain

Rubber flapper
Valve seat

25

Unclog a Toilet

Tools: Plunger, closet auger or trap and drain auger

Most toilet backups are caused by clogs in the toilet itself. The most likely place is in the trap, located just beyond the opening in the bottom of the toilet.

1) Use plunger to loosen clog in trap

Place the rubber cup directly over the outlet opening in the bottom of the toilet. Press the handle down slowly and pull up quickly. (*Illustration A.*) Repeat this several times, then remove the plunger and pour water into the bowl. If the water level does not rise considerably, the trap may be clear; test it by flushing the toilet. If the toilet flushes freely, wait and flush it again; then resume normal use.

2) Use closet auger or trap and drain auger to loosen clog

If the water still backs up, buy a closet auger, a long-handled tool that you can easily feed into the toilet. You can also use a trap and drain auger. Put the coil end of the cable into the drain hole of the toilet; push and turn the crank handle clockwise to feed around the corner and up into the bowl's trap. (*Illustration B.*)

The most common toilet is the "jet" type with its outlet opening at the rear of the bowl. Thread the auger up this opening toward the back.

3) Thread auger to front of wash-down toilet

You might have a "wash-down" type that has its outlet opening angled toward the front of the toilet, along with a smaller inlet opening at the rear. Push the auger up the larger front opening.

When you reach the obstruction, continue to turn the auger clockwise as you pull it out. (*Illustration C.*) The obstruction should come out hooked to the auger end. If you're unsuccessful at doing this, crank the coil back and forth to try to break up the obstruction. Flush the toilet. If the toilet drains, the clog has been loosened.

If the problem persists, call a plumber. The stoppage is farther along the drain and a professional is needed.

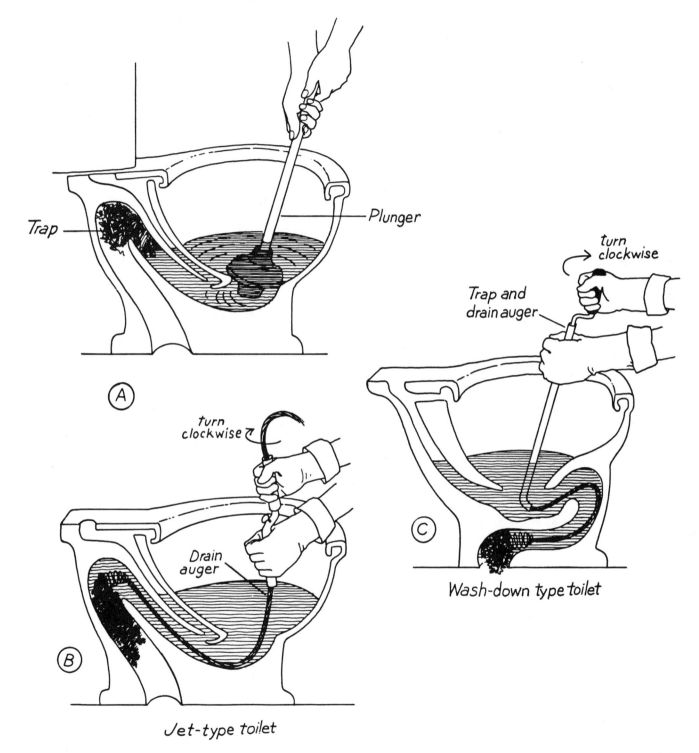

Trap

Plunger

A

turn clockwise

Trap and drain auger

C

Wash-down type toilet

turn clockwise

Drain auger

B

Jet-type toilet

27

Fix a Leaky Pipe

Tools: General-purpose scissors, screwdriver, putty knife, wire brush

A leaky pipe can be a real disaster. Water can do untold damage if left to run unchecked. Most pipe leaks, except for frozen pipes, develop slowly; the pipe rusts or corrodes and a weak spot develops. Eventually the water breaks through the weak spot and a pinhole leak results. This type of leak can be stopped, but the repair is only a temporary cure as other leaks will probably develop. If you are constantly fixing small leaks, seek professional help before one of your old pipes bursts.

Whatever the type of leak you have, you should first stop the water flow by turning off your house's main shut-off valve (see pages 8–9). Drain the water from the pipes by opening all the hot and cold water faucets on the first and second floors of your house to allow air to enter the water system. Then open all the faucets in the basement to allow the water to drain out.

1) Use hose clamp and patch on pinhole leak

To temporarily stop a small pinhole leak, use heavy-duty scissors to cut a patch from a piece of rubber (bicycle tube, kitchen glove) about 1″ square. Wrap the rubber around the pipe and hold it tight against the pipe with a hose clamp. (*Illustration A.*) Check that the hose clamp is directly over the hole before you tighten the clamp screw with a screwdriver. Use a 1″ clamp for a 1/2″-diameter pipe and a 1 1/2″ clamp for a 3/4″-diameter pipe.

2) Use pipe clamp for larger leak

To make a more permanent repair for a small leak (until the pipe rusts through in another spot) or to stop a split up to 1″ in the pipe, use a pipe repair clamp. You'll find it in the plumbing department of a hardware store or home center. First, thoroughly dry the pipe and place a rubber patch over the leak. Loosen the clamp screws with a screwdriver and fit the pipe clamp over the patch; then retighten the screws. (*Illustration B.*)

3) Use epoxy paste to repair leaking pipe joint

Stop a small drip from a pipe joint with epoxy paste. You can buy this two-part mixture at any hardware store or home center. Ask for epoxy paste or putty, not epoxy glue.

Wait until all the water stops dripping from the pipe; then dry the joint with rags. Clean any dirt or buildup of minerals from the pipe threads and joint fitting with a wire brush or steel-wool pad. Mix the epoxy according to the manufacturer's directions and apply it to the leaky area, with a putty knife. (*Illustration C.*) If you are not certain where the leak is coming from, pack the epoxy all around the joint and fitting, extending the patch several inches in both directions.

Allow the epoxy to set for at least as long as the directions suggest. Turn on the water. If the pipe continues to leak, look for professional help.

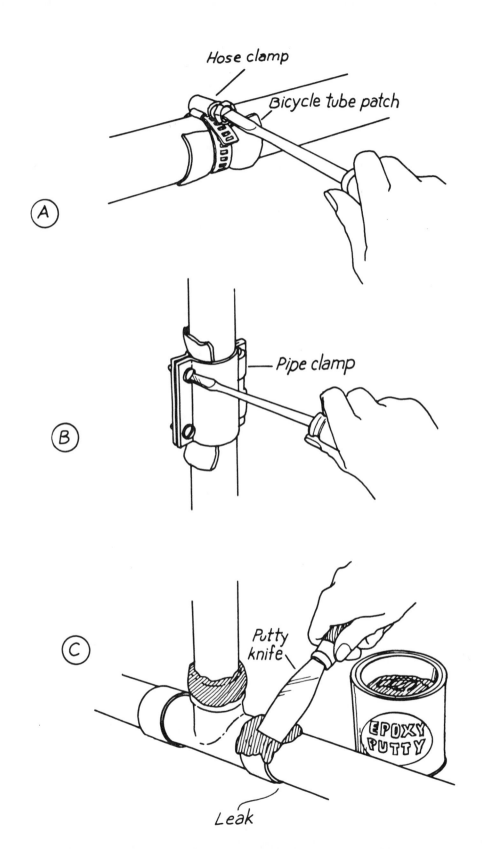

Hose clamp

Bicycle tube patch

(A)

Pipe clamp

(B)

Putty knife

(C)

EPOXY PUTTY

Leak

29

Silence Noisy Pipes

After turning the water off in your house, do you notice a loud hammering sound? Here's how to remedy it. Most plumbing systems have short sections of pipe filled with air, called air chambers, that cushion the water as it flows inside the pipes. (*See illustration.*) Through the years these air chambers fill with water and their cushioning effect is lost, which results in a loud noise when you turn off the water faucet suddenly.

Noisy water pipes can usually be silenced by draining the system, thus allowing air to reenter the pipes' air chambers.

1) Close main shut-off water valve

Turn off the main shut-off valve that stops water from entering the system (see pages 8-9).

2) Open all faucets to drain system

Open the basement faucets first, then work your way upstairs if you have a second floor. Don't forget the showers and tub faucets. Leave all faucets halfway open.

3) Close basement faucets and turn on water

Close the basement faucets and turn on the water. Go upstairs and as the water begins to come out of the faucets, turn them off and flush the toilets. Then go to the second floor's faucets; turn them off and flush the toilets.

If recharging the air chambers in your plumbing system doesn't quiet the pipes, then you could have a pipe that is not properly secured to the wall framing. These are hard to find, especially if the noise seems to come from within a wall, so call a plumber.

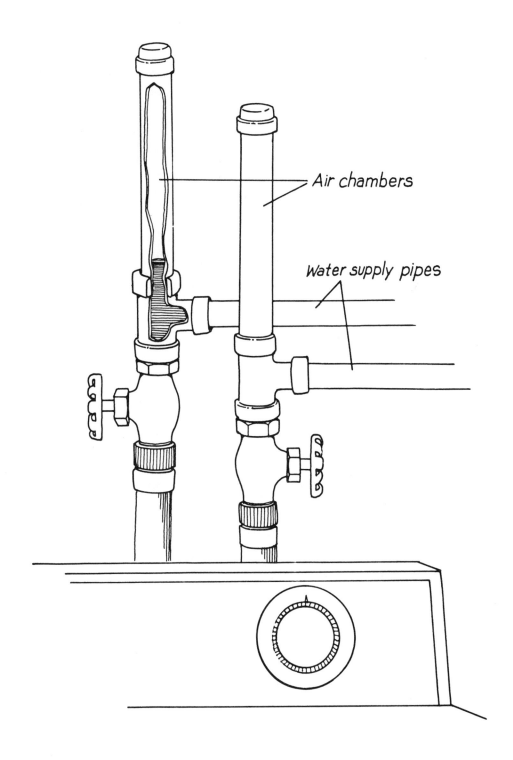

Air chambers

Water supply pipes

Unfreeze Frozen Pipes

Tools: Hair dryer, heat lamp or propane torch

A sudden drop in the temperature and your faucets don't work? When these two events coincide, it can only mean one thing—a frozen water pipe.

Apply heat to the pipe

Open the faucet so any steam from the melting ice will have an escape vent. Apply heat to the pipe, starting at the faucet and working to the frozen area. Use a hair dryer, heat lamp, heating pad, or propane torch. (Be sure to place a heatproof pad behind the pipe to protect the wall when using a torch.) Another tried-and-true solution (although a messy one) is to wrap the frozen pipe in rags and protect the area underneath with a basin; then pour boiling water over it.

You can stop heating the pipe as soon as you see or hear water running through it. Check the pipe for any splits or leaks. Some will not show up until you turn off the water at the faucet and the pressure builds in the pipe. If you have a leak, see the repair on pages 28–29. Allow the water to run; it will melt any remaining ice in the pipe.

If the weather is expected to remain cold for several days, allow the water to trickle through the pipe so it cannot freeze again. (See also pages 34–35.)

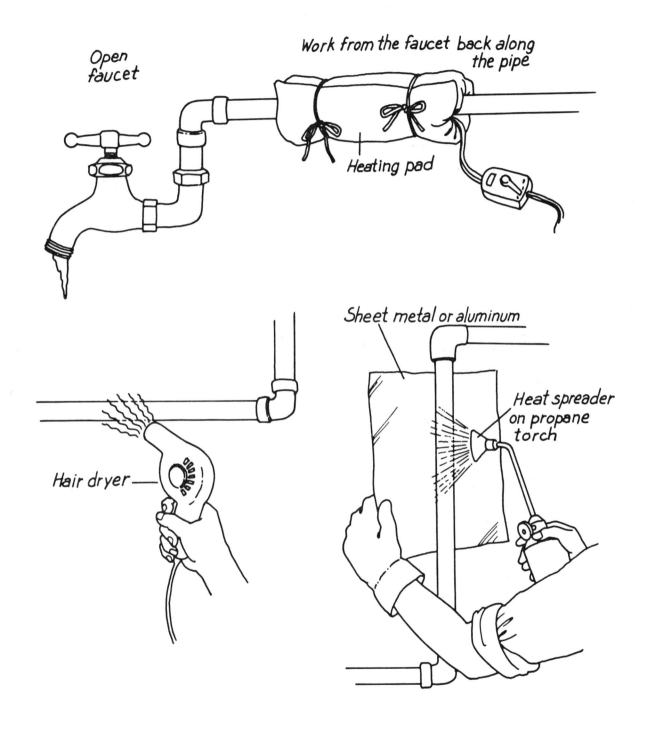

Open faucet

Work from the faucet back along the pipe

Heating pad

Hair dryer

Sheet metal or aluminum

Heat spreader on propane torch

33

Fix Sweaty Pipes or Prevent Freezing Pipes

Tools: General-purpose scissors, saw

The repair to prevent sweaty or frozen pipes is basically the same as to unfreeze frozen pipes: wrap them with insulation. This protection will also reduce heat loss from hot-water pipes and save energy as well.

Use self-sticking tape for easy installation

Pipe insulation comes in a variety of forms and the self-sticking tape is the easiest type to use. Simply wind the putty-like tape or adhesive-backed foam around pipes in a spiral fashion. Use scissors to cut and customize it to fit in various situations.

Use tubular foam insulation for most efficiency

Other types of pipe insulation are plastic foam, wool felt or fiberglass jackets that split so they slip over straight pipe sections. To cut these jackets to size, use a hacksaw or any fine-toothed saw. Seal all joints with duct tape.

Use heat tape to prevent frozen pipes

If your pipes extend through an unheated crawl space, or are in uninsulated walls or kitchen cabinets, insulation may not be enough to keep them from freezing in very cold conditions. One solution is to wrap the pipes with electric heating tape designed to protect the pipes from freezing. Read the label carefully before purchasing heat tape. Some types cannot be installed under insulation. The tape wraps around the pipes and is plugged into an outlet. Most types include a thermostat that turns the tape on automatically when the temperature drops below freezing.

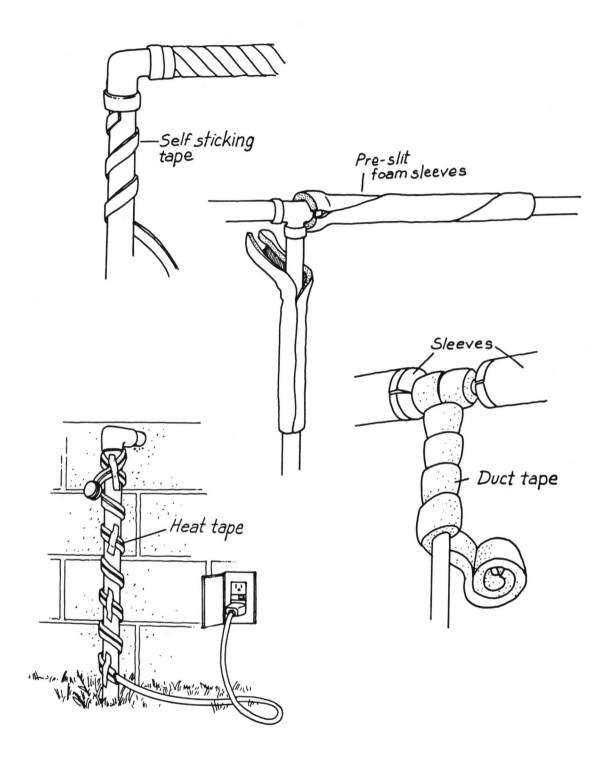

Self sticking
tape

Pre-slit
foam sleeves

Sleeves

Heat tape

Duct tape

SECTION 2

Electrical Repairs

Electrical Box Maintenance

Materials: Marking pen, pressure-sensitive labels

Before you experience an electrical problem it's a good idea for you to understand the basic elements of your main electrical panel. It is usually located in the basement, utility room or closet of houses, and near the entrance of apartments.

Opening the panel door and touching the fuses or circuit-breaker switches is not dangerous, but wherever there is electricity there is potential danger. When changing fuses or resetting circuit breakers, for your safety, check to see that the floor is dry and keep one hand at your side or in your pocket to prevent your coming in contact with a metal object and grounding you. (Also see pages 40–41 for precautions to take when handling fuses.)

1) Check for circuit breakers or fuses

You should know if your service panel has circuit breakers or fuses. Open the door and look at the panel. If you see rows of switches, you have a panel with modern circuit breakers and you will not have to purchase any replacements. The circuit breakers can be reset if they are opened or tripped by a short. If the panel has rows of round glass windows, then it is an older fuse-type panel. For information on replacing burned-out or old fuses, see pages 40–41.

2) Identify branch circuits and label them, if needed

After you have identified the type of service box you have, look on the back of the panel door and check to see if there is a list of areas that each fuse or circuit services. If there is a list, check to see that it's accurate; many times wiring changes are made and not recorded on this circuit list.

Turn on all lights, then push the circuit breaker switch to the "off" position or turn the fuse counterclockwise; have a helper tell you where the power went off. You should prepare a label stating the location (kitchen, bathroom, etc.) and stick it on the panel next to the fuse or circuit breaker, if it's not already recorded there.

3) Purchase replacement fuses, if needed

A burned-out fuse cannot be reused, so you need a supply of replacement fuses handy at all times. The amperage rating of a fuse (how much electricity it can handle) is marked on its face. Most of the fuses in your panel should have a 15-ampere rating. Circuits to the furnace, kitchen or laundry room may have 20-ampere or larger fuses. Buy a box of each ampere fuse. Keep these near the fuse box along with a flashlight.

You should also purchase several cartridge-type fuses that are used as main fuses and protect the panel from overload. They are located behind the two disconnect handles at the top of the panel. Pulling both handles, one at a time, straight out turns off all the electricity in the house, so pull the disconnect handles only during the day or if you have a flashlight handy. Check the rating of the cartridge fuses and purchase several of the same type and amperage rating.

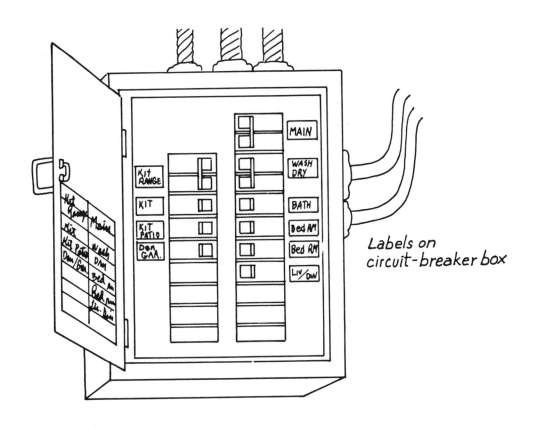

Labels on circuit-breaker box

Labels on fuse box

Change a Fuse

Tools: Fuse puller, pliers

Electric power comes into a house through a main service panel or "fuse box" usually located in the basement or utility room. These are safety devices designed to prevent an overload. As a safety precaution, don't change fuses with wet or sweaty hands or while standing on a wet floor. Use only one hand to remove fuses and touch only the glass rim of the fuse. Don't touch anything with your other hand. For extra safety, wear a rubber glove. If you are removing a cartridge fuse, use a fuse puller or pliers.

CARTRIDGE FUSES

1) Locate cartridge-type fuse

Cartridge-type fuses are located behind the main shut-off panels of the fuse box. To find out the type of cartridge fuses you have, pull the cartridge panel straight out by the handle. Use your fingers or a pliers to pull the old fuses out of the clips that hold their ends.

2) Replace cartridge with same type

Take the old fuses to a hardware store and purchase several new fuses of the exact same type. There are two types of cartridge fuses: those rated up to and including 60 amps have caps at each end of the cartridge; those over 60-amp capacity have flat copper bars sticking out of their ends. Replace the cartridge fuse by pushing it securely into the end clips of the cartridge panel.

PLUG FUSES

1) Locate blown plug-type fuse

Blown fuses are usually easy to find. Look through the center window of the electrical box; if you see a burn mark or a strip of metal that has a break in it, the fuse is blown. Usually a short circuit causes the fuse element to melt almost instantly, causing the burn behind the glass window. For a fuse that is overloaded (when too many appliances or lights are plugged into a circuit), it takes longer for the fuse element to melt, so all you'll see is the broken ribbon of wire. Short circuits and overloads must be corrected or the fuses will continue to blow.

2) Replace fuse with same type and amperage

You can expect to find three possible types of plug fuses in the box. The most common is the standard *glass plug fuse;* it has a screw-in base that looks like that on a light bulb. You can see the fusible link just behind the glass window. They come in 15-, 20-, 25-, and 30-amp sizes.

The second type of plug fuse you are likely to encounter is the *time-delay fuse.* It has the same base as the plug fuse and comes in the same amperage sizes. You can identify this fuse by the spring visible behind the window. Time-delay fuses can be substituted for plug fuses.

The third type of plug fuse you may find is the *S-type fuse.* It has a narrow threaded base and fits into a special insert screwed into the fuse box. Each size of S-type fuse has a different base; you can only thread a 15-amp S-type fuse into a 15-amp adapter and a 20-amp S-type fuse into a 20-amp adapter, and so on.

Whatever type of fuse you have, turn it counterclockwise to remove it. Replace the fuse with a fuse of the same amperage rating. If you are always blowing a plug-type fuse in the kitchen, then substitute a time-delay fuse of the same rating. Do not replace a fuse with one of a larger amperage because you will create a fire hazard.

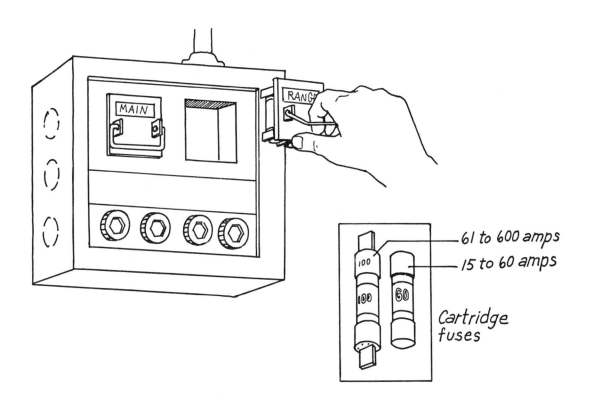

MAIN

RANGE

61 to 600 amps
15 to 60 amps

100

100

60

Cartridge fuses

Insert half remains in fuse box

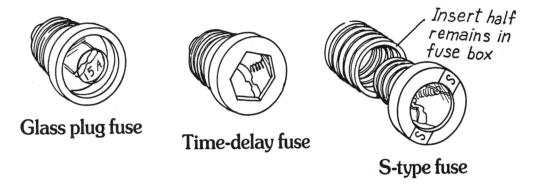

15 A

S

S

Glass plug fuse

Time-delay fuse

S-type fuse

Help! No Power!

A total blackout can be caused by two things. First, and probably the most likely cause, especially during bad weather, is a power failure with the local electric utility company. The other cause could be a blown main fuse or open main circuit breaker (see pages 38–39).

1) Check for local power failure

If all your lights go out, your hair dryer stops working or the air conditioner turns off at the same time, first look out the window to see if yours is the only home with no power. If you cannot see lights in neighbors' windows, it's likely to be a widespread power outage. There is not much you can do but wait until power is restored. It is all right to leave the lights on but turn off any appliance like a hair dryer, mixer or vacuum cleaner, because it will start up as soon as the power resumes. Resist the temptation to open the refrigerator, and especially the freezer; your food will keep longer if the door is not opened.

If the neighborhood has power and you are in the dark, then the problem is with the power lines leading into your home or with the main fuse or circuit breaker. New homes have circuit breakers, but many older homes have circuits protected by fuses. You can tell the type of protection you have by opening the main power panel. If there are rows of small round glass windows, you have fuses; if you see rows of switches, you have circuit breakers.

2) Replace cartridge for blown main fuse

The main fuses of the older type panel are located inside the two black plastic boxes at the top of the panel. Pull the handle labeled "Main," attached to the fuse box, straight out. (*Illustration A.*) The front of the box will come out of the panel.

On the back of the box front you will find two cartridge fuses. These are held in place by clips at each end. Grab the fuse in the center and pull it out of the clips. (*Illustration B.*) Replace both fuses with ones of the same capacity (amperage rating).

After you have changed the fuses, replace the box front. If the lights don't come on, check that you have pushed it in completely. If the lights come on and then go off, the fuse has probably blown again and a serious short exists in the system, so call an electrician.

3) Reset main circuit breaker

On modern power panels the main circuit breaker is located at the top, centered between the rows of branch circuit breakers and usually labeled "Main." To reset this breaker, turn it off, then back on. (*Illustration C.*) The lights should go on; if they don't, try resetting the breaker again. If the lights go on and then you hear the breaker snap, there is a serious short in the wiring and you should call an electrician.

4) Check wires between utility pole and house

If after you have replaced the main fuses or reset the main circuit for your home you still do not have power, you may wish to check the wires leading from the utility pole into the house. If you can see that there is a wire down, do not approach it. Keep everyone, including pets, away from the wire. Don't touch any metal objects on the outside of your house, like gutters or downspouts. Call the emergency service number of your local utility company immediately and report the situation.

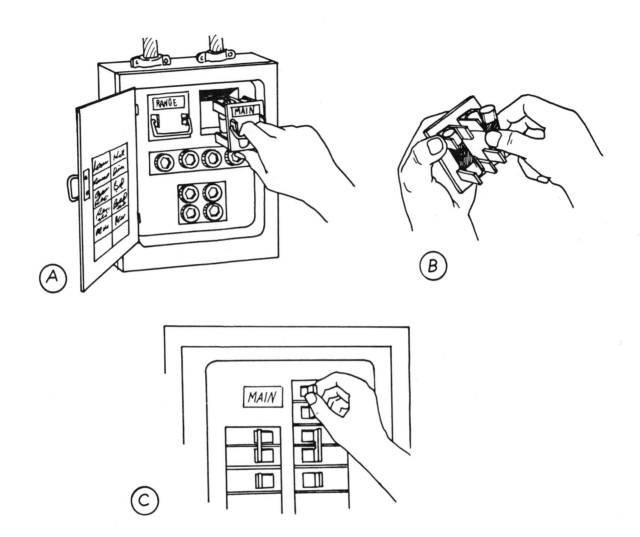

Replace a Faulty Switch

Tools: Screwdriver, electrical tape, long-nose pliers

When you turn on a light in your home and hear a buzzing noise from the switch, see the lights flicker or even see sparks fly, you can be sure the wall switch is going bad. Replacing a bad switch is easy; in most cases only six screws have to be loosened. But before you begin any electrical repair, turn the electricity off at the main electrical panel in your home by pulling the "Main" handle out of the fuse box or turning off the main circuit breaker switch (see pages 38–39).

1) Remove switch plate and switch

Whether you have a single switch or several in a single electrical box, replacing the bad switch is the same. Remove the switch plate cover by loosening the two switch plate screws with a screwdriver. Next, remove the two screws at the top and bottom of the switch that hold it to the electrical box in the wall and pull the faulty switch out of the box. (*Illustration A.*)

2) Remove wires and tape wire ends

Before you disconnect any wires, draw a sketch of the switch and mark the location of all wires. Then remove the wires and wrap electrical tape around the bare ends of each wire. Push the wires back into the box and reinstall the switch plate cover.

It is safe to turn the electricity on while you take the faulty switch to your local hardware store or home center and purchase a replacement.

3) Replace wires and install new switch

Before you begin to install the new switch, check that the electricity is off. Install the wires on the new switch in the reverse order you removed them from the bad switch. The black wire should be connected to the brass-colored screw, and a white or colored wire (but not the green wire) to the silver-colored screw. Make sure that the wire loop curls in the same direction, clockwise, and that the screw turns when it is being tightened. (*Illustration B.*) Use a long-nose pliers to bend the wire around the switch's terminal screws.

If your new switch has a green ground terminal screw and the old one didn't, attach a short wire to this terminal. Hook the other end of the short wire to the bare wire or the green ground wire in the box. (*Illustration C.*) If there is no bare or green wire, then connect the short wire to one of the screws that holds the switch in the box.

Push the new switch back into the box; install the two screws that hold the switch in the electrical box; then reinstall the switch cover plate.

Single pole ungrounded switch

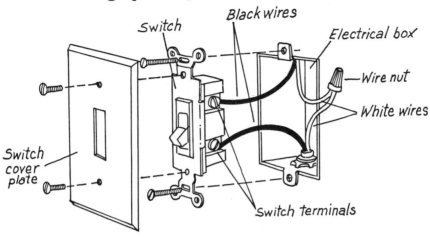

Switch

Black wires

Electrical box

Wire nut

White wires

Switch cover plate

Switch terminals

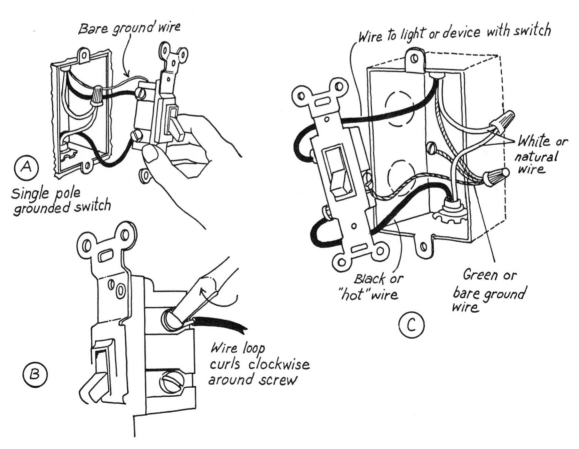

Bare ground wire

Wire to light or device with switch

White or natural wire

(A)

Single pole grounded switch

Black or "hot" wire

Green or bare ground wire

(C)

(B)

Wire loop curls clockwise around screw

Replace a Faulty Outlet

Tools: Screwdriver, electrical tape, long-nose pliers

Electrical outlets wear out and can cause a short circuit or lights to blink on and off or appliances to run intermittently. Replacing the outlet is easy; in most cases only a few screws have to be loosened. But before you begin any electrical repair, turn off the electricity at the main electrical panel in your home. Pull the "Main" handle on the fuse box or turn off the main circuit-breaker switch (see pages 38–39).

1) Remove outlet cover plate and outlet

Whether you have a single outlet or several in a single electrical box, replacing the bad outlet is the same. Remove the outlet cover plate by loosening the outlet plate screw(s) with a screwdriver. Next, remove the two screws at the top and bottom of the outlet in the wall and pull the faulty outlet out of the box.

2) Remove wires and tape wire ends

Take a good look at the outlet. Before you disconnect any wires, draw a sketch of the outlet and mark the location of all wires. Then remove the wires and wrap electrical tape around the bare ends of each wire. Push the wires back into the box and reinstall the outlet cover plate.

It is safe to turn the electricity on while you take the faulty outlet to your local hardware store or home center and purchase a replacement.

3) Replace wires and install new outlet

Before you begin to install the new outlet, check that the electricity is off. Install the wires on the new outlet in the reverse order you removed them from the bad outlet. The black wire should be connected to the brass-colored screw, and the white wire to the silver-colored screw. Make sure that the wire loop curls in the same direction, clockwise, that the screw turns when it is being tightened. (*Illustration A.*) Use a long-nose pliers to bend the wire around the terminal screws.

If your new outlet has a green ground terminal screw and the old one didn't, attach a short wire to this terminal and to the green or bare ground wire in the box. (*Illustration B.*) If there is no bare or green wire, then connect the short wire to one of the screws that holds the switch in the box.

Push the outlet back into the box; install the two screws that hold the outlet in the electrical box; then reinstall the outlet cover plate.

Old double electrical outlet

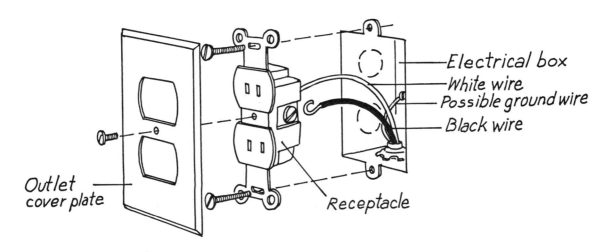

Electrical box

White wire
Possible ground wire

Black wire

Outlet
cover plate

Receptacle

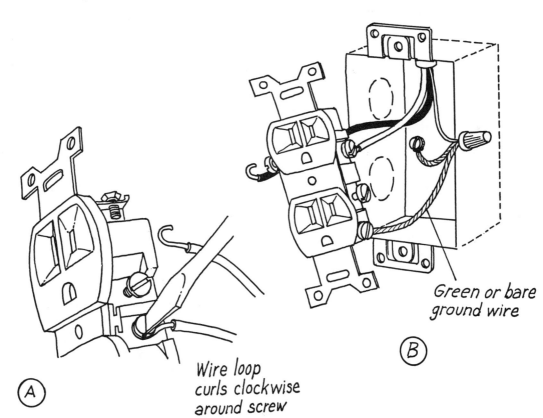

Green or bare
ground wire

Wire loop
curls clockwise
around screw

Ⓐ

Ⓑ

Replace a Ceiling or Wall Fixture

Tools: Screwdriver, long-nose pliers

When the ceiling fixture in a room doesn't work or you want to replace it with a new one, the most difficult part of the job is doing the repair while you're up on a ladder. This is a good two-person job so you're not making countless trips up and down. The wiring is easy; in most cases only a black wire and white wire are involved. Before you begin working on the fixture, turn off all electricity at the main electrical panel in your home (see pages 38–39). Remove any glass diffuser globe or shade, and then the bulb.

Replace fixture attached directly to electrical box
(*Illustration A*)

Most porcelain single-bulb utility fixtures like those found in closet lights are attached to the electrical box with two screws that are screwed directly into the box ears. With a screwdriver, remove the screws and lower the fixture from the box. Untwist the wire nuts holding the black and white fixture wires and supply wires in the electrical box together. If the supply wires are attached to terminal screws, loosen the screws and remove the wires.

Purchase a new fixture, checking at the hardware store or home center that the one you buy will fit the previous attaching hardware. If any adapters are needed, get them before you take the fixture home.

Install the new fixture by reversing the order that you removed the parts of the old one. Make sure you connect the black wire to the brass-colored terminal on the fixture and the white wire to the silver-colored terminal. If the fixture is prewired, connect the black and white and green wires to the same colored wires in the ceiling box.

Replace fixture connected to fixture strap
(*Illustration B*)

If you have a strap-mounted fixture, remove the two screws holding the cover or canopy to the fixture strap and carefully lower it away from the ceiling. Remove the plastic wire nuts or unwrap the electrical tape that holds the black and white fixture wires to the supply wires in the electrical box.

You can leave the old fixture strap in place if it is the same size as the one supplied with your new fixture; otherwise replace the old strap with the new one. Follow the manufacturer's installation instructions to connect the fixture wires to the supply wires. Twist the black wires together with the pliers, then screw on the wire nut. Do the same to the white wires. Connect the green ground wires together; or if there is no green wire in the electrical box, connect the green fixture wire to the bare wire or to one of the screws holding the fixture to the electrical box.

Replace stud-mounted fixture (*Illustrations C*)

Most heavy fixtures and chandeliers are attached to a stud coming out of the center of the electrical ceiling box. Have a helper hold the fixture, or set it on your ladder to take its weight off the suspension chain. Then loosen the ring called the "collar" that holds the cover tight against the ceiling. Lower the fixture away from the ceiling and remove the wire nuts or electrical tape that holds the fixture and supply wires together. Straighten the ends of the fixture wires so they will pass down the nipple (threaded rod).

The length of the old nipple can be adjusted an inch or so by screwing it into the hickey (the U-shaped bracket the nipple is threaded into), but allow room for the wires. You can purchase longer or shorter nipples at the hardware store or home center.

Install the new fixture according to the manufacturer's directions. Connect the black and white wires together and twist them tight with a long-nose pliers. Then install the wire nuts. Attach the green ground wires together in the same way. If there is no green wire in the box, attach the green fixture wire to the bare wire or to a screw inside the electrical box.

Screw the canopy back in place; install new light bulbs; and turn on the electricity in the room again.

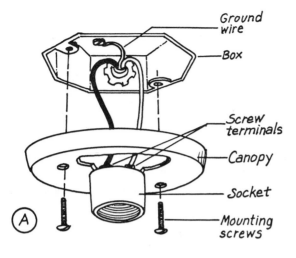

Ground wire

Box

Screw terminals

Canopy

Socket

Mounting screws

(A)

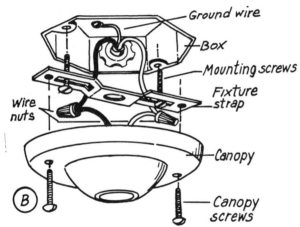

Ground wire

Box

Mounting screws

Fixture strap

Wire nuts

Canopy

Canopy screws

(B)

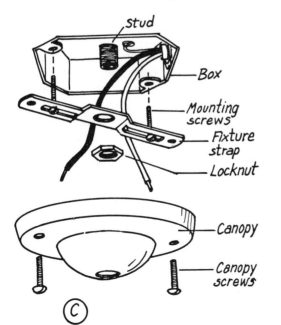

Stud

Box

Mounting screws

Fixture strap

Locknut

Canopy

Canopy screws

(C)

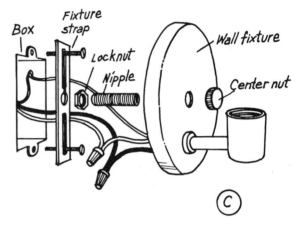

Box

Fixture strap

Locknut

Nipple

Wall fixture

Center nut

(C)

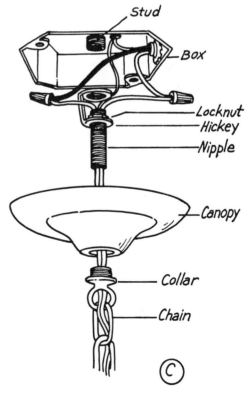

Stud

Box

Locknut

Hickey

Nipple

Canopy

Collar

Chain

(C)

49

Replace a Plug

Tools: Wire cutter (multipurpose electrical tool), screwdriver

Plugs wear out, especially if you pull them out of the wall by the cord. They also become unreliable if they are constantly overloaded (servicing several electrical fixtures or appliances) and become hot. There are three basic types of plugs used around your home: 1) lightweight snap-on plugs used on lamps; 2) two-prong light-duty plugs used on lamps and extension cords; and 3) heavy-duty grounded plugs for appliances and extension cords. All can be easily replaced.

Replace a snap-on plug

Snap-on plugs are easy to remove—just pull up on the clamp lever and the cord will pull out of the plug body.

To replace a snap-on plug, cut the end of the cord clean with a wire cutter, leaving no frayed wire ends. Lift the clamp and slip the cord end into the slot in the plug. Then push the clamp tight against the wire until the clamp lever is flush with the plug body. The plug is ready to use.

Replace a two-prong plug

Unplug the cord before working on the plug. To replace a traditional two-prong plug, remove the insulating case by inserting the tip of your screwdriver between the plug body and case and prying the two apart. Loosen the screws to free the wires and remove the plug. You might have to untie the wires to pull them through the plug case if an underwriter's knot (as illustrated) was used.

Purchase a plug at least as heavy as the one you are replacing. If the insulation at the end of the wire is brittle, cut it off with a wire cutter and strip about 1/2″ of insulation from the end of each wire. If the insulation is flexible, just twist the loose strands of wire together.

Thread the cord wires into the new plug body and tie an underwriter's knot in the cord. This knot prevents the cord from being pulled out of the plug. With your screwdriver, loosen the screws on the plug body and wind the ends of the cord around each terminal screw in a clockwise direction (the same way the screw tightens). Tighten each terminal screw and check that there are no loose wire strands sticking out that might cause a short. Pull the cord through the body until the knot jams; then tuck the wires into the cover and push the plug body into the cover until it snaps tight.

Replace a grounded heavy-duty three-prong plug

This type of plug is found at the end of heavy-duty extension cords, appliances, and power tools. Changing this type of plug is no different than the two-prong plug. The plug body could be held together by several screws found in the face of the plug end. Loosen these screws; otherwise, just slide the plug cover to expose the screw terminals. Loosen the terminal screws and remove the wires from the plug body. You might have to loosen the cord clamp. Take the plug cover and plug to the hardware store or home center to purchase a replacement.

Install the new plug by reversing the order that you removed the old one. Thread the end of the wire into the plug. Tie the wire ends into an underwriter's knot and twist the wire strands at the ends of the wires together. Then wind them around the terminal screws (clockwise) to prevent loose strands of wire from shorting against one another. Connect the black wire to the brass-colored screw and the white wire to the silver-colored screw. The green ground wires should go around the green terminal screw. Put the plug cover in place. If there is a cord clamp, tighten it with a screwdriver.

SNAP-ON PLUG

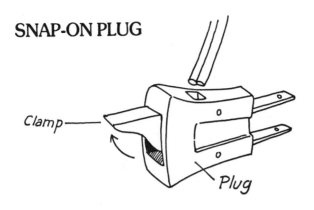

Clamp

Plug

TWO-PRONG PLUG

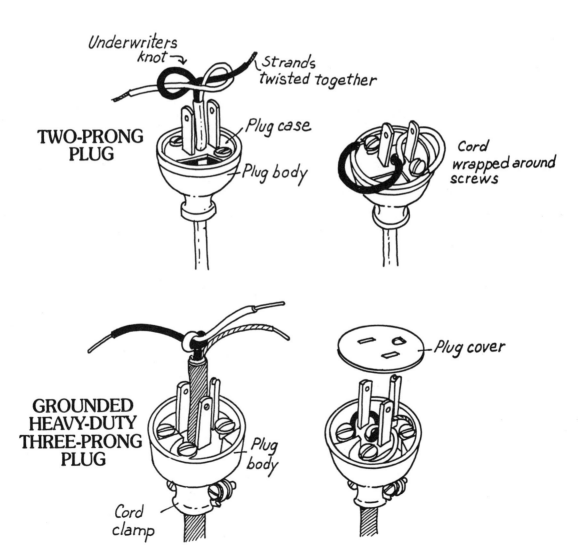

Underwriters knot

Strands twisted together

Plug case

Plug body

Cord wrapped around screws

GROUNDED HEAVY-DUTY THREE-PRONG PLUG

Plug cover

Plug body

Cord clamp

Fix an Extension Cord

Tools: Wire cutter, utility knife or wire stripper, electrical tape

Sometime your hedge trimmer or electric lawn mower may have an encounter with its extension cord, causing the appliance to stop in a shower of sparks. All is not lost. Fixing an extension cord is easy. First, unplug the extension cord.

1) Cut away damaged cord

Use a wire cutter to cut off the damaged section of cord. Remove 2 inches of the *outer* covering from each end of the cord. Be careful not to cut the insulation around each individual wire.

2) Splice like-colored wires

Strip an inch of insulation from each wire with a wire stripper or sharp knife. Twist the ends of like-colored wires tightly together. Wrap each splice with electrical tape. Then wrap the entire area with electrical tape, overlapping the splice area by several inches to give the cord strength.

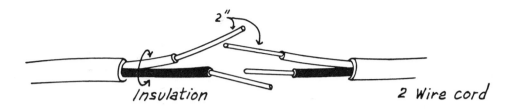

2"

Insulation

2 Wire cord

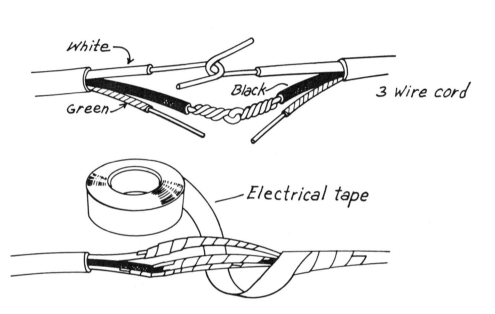

White

Black

Green

3 Wire cord

Electrical tape

Rewire a Lamp

Tools: Screwdriver, utility knife, wire cutter

The easiest quick-fix for a nonworking lamp is to check the light bulb. Is it burned out or loose in the socket? Also check to see that the plug is securely inserted into the wall outlet. If the lamp still doesn't light, then here's how to fix it.

1) Inspect cord and plug

Unplug the lamp before working on it. Inspect the cord and plug; if the cord shows no sign of wear and the insulation is flexible, then inspect the plug. It should be on tight and show no signs of a short circuit (burn marks by the prongs). If both the cord and plug are all right, then the problem is most likely in the socket.

2) Open socket and check wires

Separate the outer socket shell from the cap by inserting the tip of a screwdriver into the seam between them while you press in on the shell. Pry the shell off the cap. Next, remove the cardboard insulating sleeve between the shell and the socket. The terminal screws are at the base of the socket; check that both are tight. If they are loose, tighten them, reassemble the socket, and see if the lamp works again.

3) Replace worn socket

If the lamp still doesn't work or if the cardboard insulating sleeve is charred or crumbly, replace the old socket. Loosen the set screw at the base of the cap and undo the knot in the cord. Then unscrew the cap from the end of the threaded rod that runs through the lamp.

When buying a new socket, you'll see that they are available for either standard or three-way bulbs. You can replace a standard socket with a three-way socket because they are interchangeable and the wiring is the same. To install your new socket, reverse the process used to remove the old one.

4) Replace old wire

If the lamp's cord is worn, replace it when the socket is off the lamp. Use a utility knife to remove any protective felt backing on the lamp's bottom. This gives you access to the wiring tube or shell that goes to the switch socket. After you have removed the wires from the switch terminals and untied the knot in the cord, pull the old wire out of the lamp from the bottom.

Turn the lamp upside-down and push the new wire into the tube until it comes out the other end. If it gets stuck you might have to remove the threaded tube from the lamp. Pull about a foot of wire out of the other end of the tube; then route the other end of the wire out of the lamp base in the same manner as the old wire. Tie a knot in the wire inside the lamp where the wire comes out of the base. The knot prevents the wire from being pulled out of the lamp.

Replace the bottom felt or cover of the lamp. You usually don't have to reglue the cover since the lamp rests on it. If needed, use rubber cement or a general-purpose cement to reglue the felt to a glass lamp. Use carpenter's glue to attach felt to a wood base.

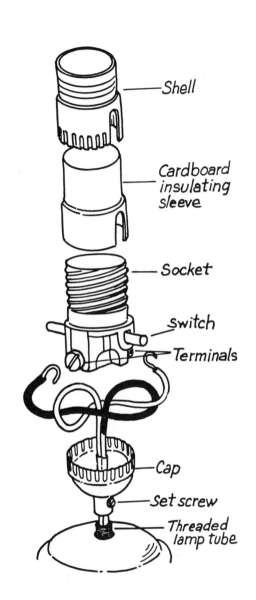

Shell

Cardboard
insulating
sleeve

Socket

Switch

Terminals

Cap

Set screw

Threaded
lamp tube

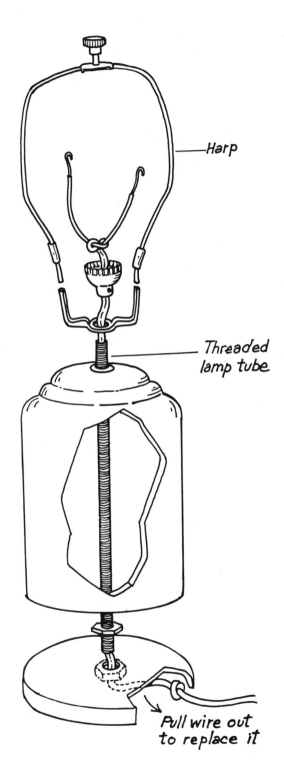

Harp

Threaded
lamp tube

Pull wire out
to replace it

Replace a Fluorescent Tube Starter

When you flip the switch and the fluorescent tube flickers but doesn't light, or just glows red at the ends, chances are that the tube or starter is going bad.

1) Check fluorescent tube and look for starter

First, turn off the light and check that the fluorescent tube is fully seated in its brackets. Twist the tube 90 degrees and slip the pins out of the bracket. Look for the starter, a small aluminum can located in the base of the fixture close to one of the tube brackets. If you don't see the starter, you probably have either an instant or rapid-start fixture without a starter.

Replace the fluorescent tube and try the light again. If it still does not light, purchase a replacement tube. If that does not solve the problem, then the ballast is at fault and you should call an electrician to replace it.

2) Remove fluorescent tube to check starter

If your fixture has a starter, remove the tube, then push the starter in and give it a twist, causing it to pop out. Some types have a reset button sticking out of the bottom. Try pushing the button in and replacing the starter and tube in the fixture. If the light doesn't work, replace the starter. If the starter has no reset button, take it to your local hardware store or home center and purchase a new starter. Install the new starter, replace the tube, and turn on the light.

You can extend the life of your fluorescent tubes by turning them on and off as little as possible, but weigh this against the additional electricity consumed.

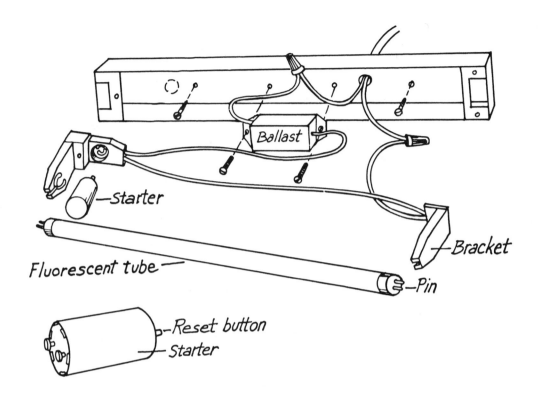

Ballast

—Starter

Fluorescent tube—

—Bracket

—Pin

—Reset button
—Starter

Telephone Troubleshooting

Tools: Screwdriver

It was not too long ago that you thought nothing of calling the telephone company when you had trouble with your phone. These days phones are a lot easier to service because the new modular designs enable you to make minor repairs on your own. Your local telephone company can send you a free booklet on repairing a modular telephone. Here are a few steps you should take before you call for service.

1) Check phone cords

If you have trouble with a modular telephone, first check its cords. Unplug the cord from the handset to the phone body and the cord from the phone to the wall jack; then reattach them. The problem might have been a loose plug.

2) Check all phones

Check to see if the trouble is with only one phone or your entire telephone system. If your other phones work, then unplug the suspect phone and try it in another location that has a suitable wall jack. If the suspect phone still does not work, take it to your local phone store for repairs.

3) Check modular plug

If the problem phone works at another location, then the trouble is probably in the phone wiring to that room. Check the modular outlet for loose wires. Open the jack or remove the cover from the junction box. There is only low telephone voltage on these wires. Use a screwdriver to tighten all screws, and check that all wires of the same color are securely attached to the terminals. Sometimes only the red and green wires are hooked to the terminals. Try the telephone again. If it does not work, call the telephone company or telephone service center for assistance.

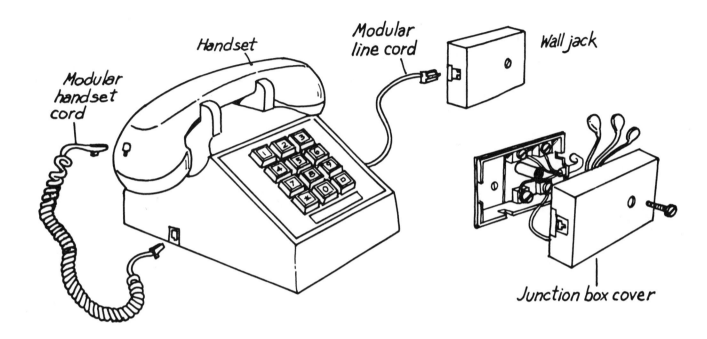

Modular handset cord

Handset

Modular line cord

Wall jack

Junction box cover

SECTION 3

Heating and Cooling Repairs

No Heat

Whether you have a gas, electric or oil furnace, it is usually very reliable. Most furnace failures occur in the fall at the start of the heating season. Many times an open safety relay or fuse is the cause of the problem. If after following these suggestions you get the furnace running, call the furnace serviceman for an annual checkup.

Checklist for an electrical heat unit
• Check that the circuit breakers or fuses serving the furnace are in working order (see pages 38–39).
• Check to see that the furnace switch is on.
• Check that the thermostat is on the heating setting if the system has central air-conditioning.
• Check a cold electric baseboard unit for open thermal cutout device. Turn the thermostat off, then remove its cover and look for a reset button. It is usually in the end compartment where wires are joined with wire nuts. Some baseboard units have their fuse located over the finned heating element. Check the reset button by pushing it in until a click is heard or until it stays in.

Checklist for an oil-burning heat unit
• Check that the circuit breakers or fuses serving the furnace are in working order (see pages 38–39).
• Check to see that the furnace's master switch is on.
• Check that the thermostat is on the heating setting if the system has central air-conditioning.
• Check the oil supply in the storage tank.
• Check the reset button on the oil-burner motor by pushing it in until a click is heard or until the button stays in.

• Check the reset button on the stack, the large pipe leading from the furnace into the chimney. Reset the button by pushing it in until you hear a click or until it stays in.

Checklist for a gas-burning heat unit
• Check that the circuit breakers or fuses serving the furnace are in working order (see pages 38–39).
• Check to see that the furnace switch is on.
• Check that the thermostat is on the heating setting if the system has central air-conditioning.
• Check that the pilot is lit. Consult your owner's manual for the location of the pilot light. You can usually see the pilot light by opening or removing the inspection panel on the side or end of the furnace. If the pilot is out, look on the furnace panels close to the pilot or in the owner's manual for specific lighting instructions.

First, turn the furnace off, then turn the knob on the combination control off, then back to pilot position; hold a button or the dial down, and light the pilot. Continue to hold the button down for about 30 seconds to heat the thermocouple, then release the button and the pilot should stay lit. If not, try again. If the pilot won't stay lit, then call a repairman.

With the pilot lit, turn the knob on the combination control to the "on" position. Turn the furnace on and the main burners should light; if not, call a repairman.
• Check the gas supply. Look at the manual shut-off valve on the furnace; it should be open (handle aligned with pipe). Is the gas heat to your building on? To find out, try another gas appliance.

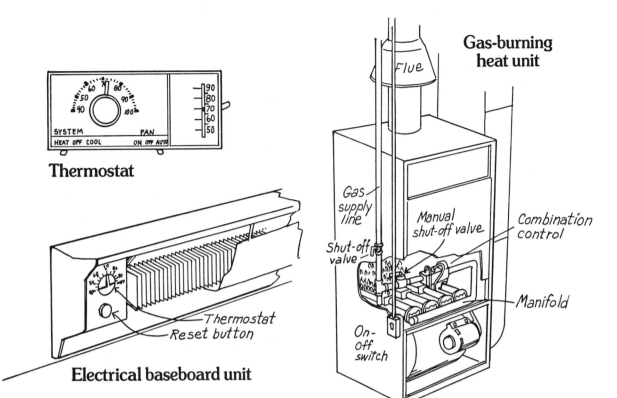

Thermostat

Gas-burning heat unit

Flue

Gas supply line

Shut-off valve

Manual shut-off valve

Combination control

Manifold

On-off switch

Thermostat
Reset button

Electrical baseboard unit

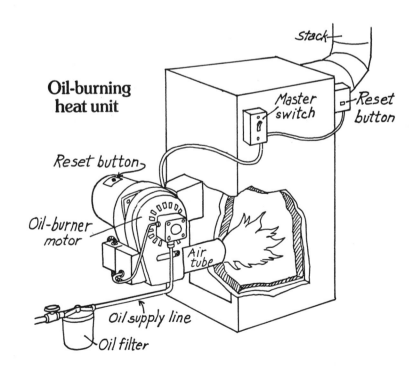

Oil-burning heat unit

Stack

Master switch

Reset button

Reset button

Oil-burner motor

Air tube

Oil supply line

Oil filter

Maintaining Your Furnace

Tools: Screwdriver

Every fall it is a good idea to have a routine check of your heating system. It does not matter whether the heat is produced by burning oil or gas or by electrical resistance; each type of furnace requires basically the same care.

It is money well spent to hire a furnace repairman to perform this routine work, especially if you have never worked on a furnace before. Arrange to be present when the work is being done so you can ask questions and become familiar with the furnace. Find out where the filter is located and how to relight the gas pilot or reset the oil-burner motor if they go out. (See pages 62–63.) Ask for a sticker with an emergency call number and post it on the furnace.

When you become familiar with your furnace, perform these basic maintenance steps.

1) Change air filter once a month in hot air system

Turn off the furnace first before you clean or change the filter. The filter is usually located inside the furnace in front of the return air duct (a large round or rectangular pipe leading to the bottom of the furnace). If the filter is fiberglass, change it once a month during the heating season. Buy a carton of filters when they're on sale.

Replace the filter by simply pulling out the old one and reinstalling a new one. Check the air flow directions on the filter. Install it so that the correct side faces the incoming air. The air should flow out of the main return duct into the furnace.

If your furnace has a metal or foam filter, it can be washed and replaced. Use warm water and a mild detergent and rinse the filter thoroughly. Let it dry overnight or use a hair dryer to make sure that it is absolutely dry before replacing it.

2) Release air from valves of radiators in hot water system

To ensure a steady, even heat, make sure that there is no buildup of air in your radiators or baseboard convectors and pipes. Release the trapped air by using a screwdriver or a radiator key to open the vent valves on the end of each radiator. Look for the valves at the end of each baseboard convector. Turn this valve counterclockwise until water comes out. Hold a cup or pan under the valve to catch the water; let the water run for a second or two, then close the valve.

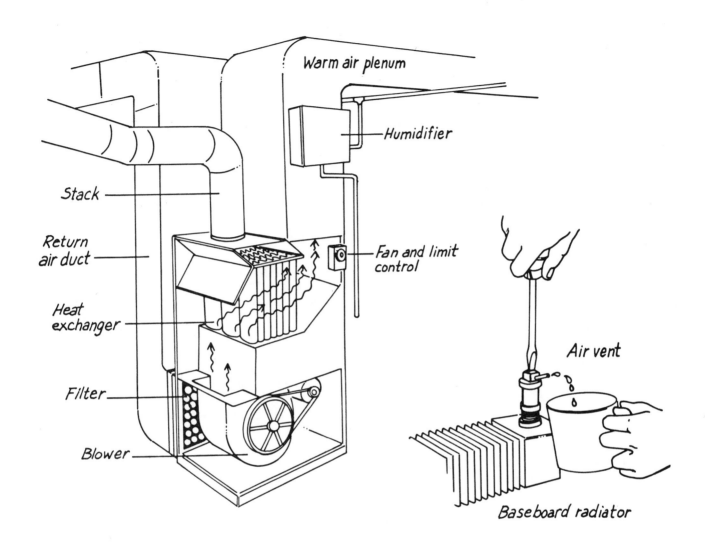

Warm air plenum

Humidifier

Stack

Return air duct

Fan and limit control

Heat exchanger

Filter

Blower

Air vent

Baseboard radiator

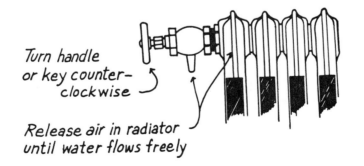

Turn handle or key counter-clockwise

Release air in radiator until water flows freely

No Hot Water

Hot water heaters are usually very reliable since they have very few moving parts. If you find yourself without hot water, run through the basic checklists below. When you find the problem, don't just correct it but investigate the cause. Most hot water heaters give you some warning signs before they quit for good. Small leaks and rusty spots on the sides of the hot water tank are sure signs of a failing water heater. A broken water heater tank will release a 30-gallon or more flood of water into your basement or utility room and produce a steady flow until the inlet valve is closed.

Gas hot water heater

• Check that the pilot is lit. Consult your owner's manual for the location of the pilot light. You can usually see the pilot light by opening or removing the inspection panel. This panel is located at the bottom of the heater tank where the gas pipes enter the side of the heater. If you don't see the pilot flame, it is out. Look on the furnace panels close to the pilot or in your owner's manual for specific lighting instructions.

In general, first you turn the knob on the control valve to "off," then back to pilot position; hold a button or the dial down, and light the pilot. Continue to hold the button down for about 30 seconds to heat the thermocouple, then release the button and the pilot should stay lit. If it does, then turn the knob to the "on" position and the main heater burner should light.

• Check the gas supply. Is the manual shut-off at the hot water heater open (handle aligned with pipe)? Is the gas heat to your building on? To find out, try another gas appliance.

• Check that the thermostat is set to at least the normal position. Try raising the temperature to see if the heater starts up.

Electric hot water heater

• Check that the circuit breakers or fuses serving the heater are in working order (see pages 38–39).

• Check that the thermostat is set to at least the normal position. Try raising the temperature to see if the heater starts up.

Oil hot water heater

• Check that the circuit breakers or fuses serving the heater are in working order (see pages 38–39).

• Check to see if the heater's master switch is on.

• Check that the thermostat is set to at least the normal position. Try raising the temperature to see if the heater starts up.

• Check the oil supply in the storage tank.

• Check the reset button on the oil burner's motor by pushing in the button until a click is heard or until the button stays in.

GAS HOT WATER HEATER

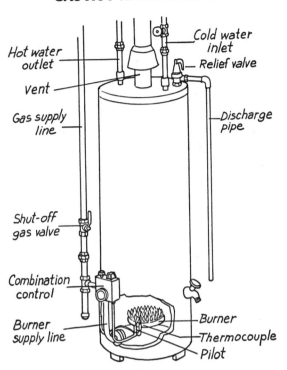

Hot water outlet

Cold water inlet

Relief valve

Vent

Gas supply line

Discharge pipe

Shut-off gas valve

Combination control

Burner supply line

Burner

Thermocouple

Pilot

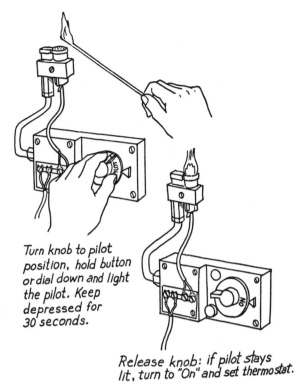

Turn knob to pilot position, hold button or dial down and light the pilot. Keep depressed for 30 seconds.

Release knob: if pilot stays lit, turn to "On" and set thermostat.

ELECTRIC HOT WATER HEATER

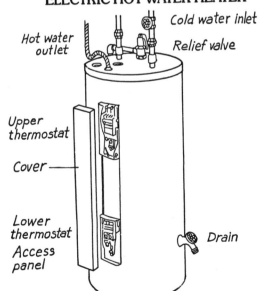

Hot water outlet

Cold water inlet

Relief valve

Upper thermostat

Cover

Lower thermostat

Access panel

Drain

OIL HOT WATER HEATER

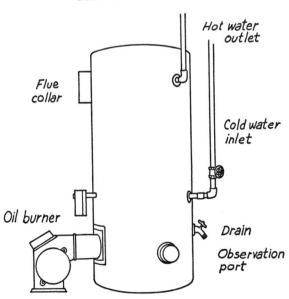

Flue collar

Hot water outlet

Cold water inlet

Oil burner

Drain

Observation port

No Air-Conditioning

Air-conditioning, once a luxury, is considered a necessity today by many people. Central air conditioners and window air-conditioning units usually run trouble-free for years. When they stop, it is usually not for a trivial reason. Here are some basic points to check if your unit stops.

Window air conditioners
- Check the air conditioner's power supply; inspect its circuit breaker in your home's electrical panel (see pages 38–39).
- Check the thermostat; turn it to a higher (colder) setting.
- Check and clean its filter (see pages 70–71).
- Check that the condensation drain is clear.

Central air-conditioning
- Check that the thermostat has been changed from "heat" to "cool." If there is a blower switch on the thermostat, push it to the "on" setting and see if the blower runs. If it does, then the fault is in the air conditioner, not the furnace.
- Check the air conditioner's power supply; inspect the circuit breaker or fuse serving the air conditioner's compressor in your home's electrical box (see pages 38–39). If the blower does not run, check that the furnace is turned on and that the furnace fuse or circuit breaker is not open.
- Check the thermostat; turn it to a higher (cooler) setting.
- Check the drain tube, which comes out of the top of the furnace, for a clog. A stopped-up drain will cause water to drip out of the furnace when the air conditioner runs on humid days.

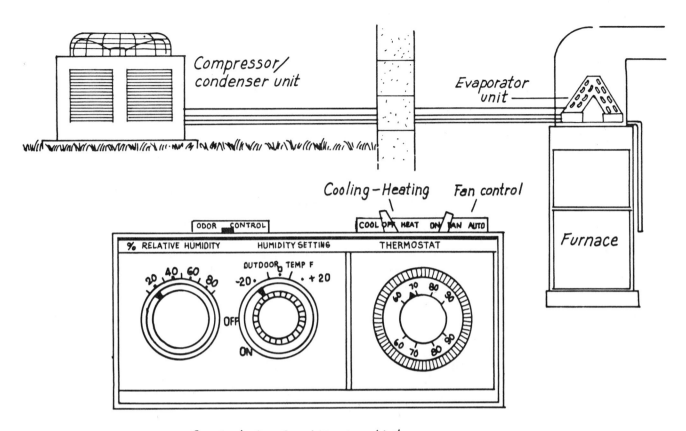

Compressor/condenser unit

Evaporator unit

Furnace

Cooling–Heating   Fan control

ODOR CONTROL

COOL OFF HEAT   ON FAN AUTO

% RELATIVE HUMIDITY   HUMIDITY SETTING   THERMOSTAT

20 40 60 80

OUTDOOR TEMP F
-20 · · · +20

OFF

ON

60 70 80 90
60 70 80 90

Central Air-Conditioning Unit

Maintaining Your Window Air Conditioner

Tools: Carpenter's level

To keep a window-unit air conditioner running smoothly and efficiently, here are a few basic tips. Unplug the unit before working on it.

1) Clean filter

At the beginning of the summer, remove and clean the air filter. It is located behind the front cover of the air conditioner. Check your owner's manual for instructions on how to remove the front cover. Wash the filter in warm water and mild detergent, then dry and replace it. Check the filter weekly and wash it as soon as any dirt accumulates.

2) Clean condenser coils

Use the crevice tool of your vacuum cleaner or a brush to clear the evaporator coils (located behind the filter) and the condenser coils at the back of the air conditioner of any accumulated dirt or dust. After your vacuum has sucked up as much dirt as possible, reverse your vacuum hose, if at all possible, and blow out any remaining dirt from around the coils.

3) Clear condensation drain

Clean the drain opening in the bottom of the air conditioner. Some models have a notch in the back of the bottom pan lip. Check that the drain is clear and that no dirt is blocking the free flow of the water that will drip off the evaporator coils on humid days. Also check that the unit is level (a carpenter's level may be used for this) or that the unit is tilted slightly down so that water will run outside.

4) Clean exterior of unit and remove shrubbery blockage

Check outside the air conditioner to see that shrubbery or tree branches do not block the passage of air into or around the unit. Air must circulate freely to cool the condenser. Trim away any tree branches or shrubbery, if necessary.

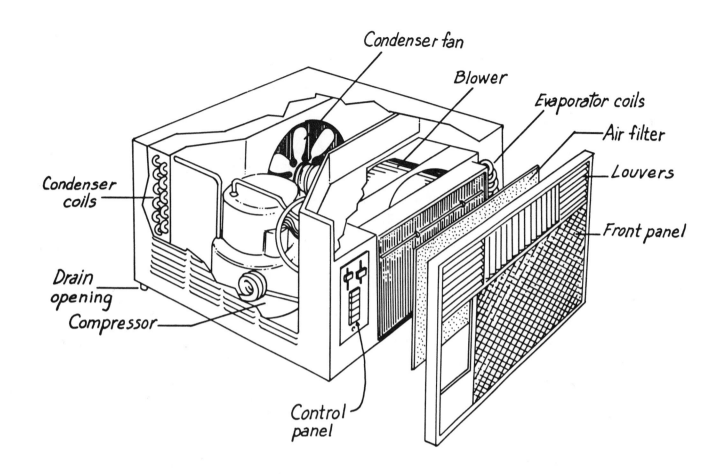

Condenser fan

Blower

Evaporator coils

Air filter

Louvers

Front panel

Condenser coils

Drain opening

Compressor

Control panel

71

Maintaining Your Central Air-Conditioning

To keep your central air conditioner running smoothly and efficiently, here are a few basic tips. Turn the power off to both the air conditioner and furnace in your house before working on the former.

1) Clean filter

At the beginning of the summer, remove and clean the air filter, located behind the front cover of the air conditioner. See your owner's manual for instructions on how to remove the front cover. Wash the filter in warm water and mild detergent, then dry and replace it. Check the filter weekly and wash it as soon as any dirt accumulates.

2) Clean evaporator coils

Use the crevice tool of your vacuum cleaner or a brush to clear the evaporator coils (located in the main duct at the top of your air conditioner) of any accumulated dirt or dust. You will have to remove the inspection cover to see the coils. They are usually in two banks that form a large A. After your vacuum has sucked up as much dirt as possible, reverse your vacuum hose, if possible, and blow out any remaining dirt.

3) Clear condensation drain

Check the drain tube coming out of the upper furnace duct. Clean any dirt or lint that might block the free flow of the water that drips off the evaporator coils on humid days. This water collects in a drip pan under the evaporator coils; if the drain is clogged, the water overflows the pan and runs inside the furnace or drips down the outside of the ducts.

4) Clean exterior of unit and remove shrubbery blockage

Check outside the air conditioner to see that shrubbery or tree branches have not overgrown the compressor unit. There must be free passage of air into or around the unit to cool the condenser. Trim away any tree branches or shrubbery, if necessary. Also clean out any leaves, paper or other debris that might be lodged in or around the compressor unit.

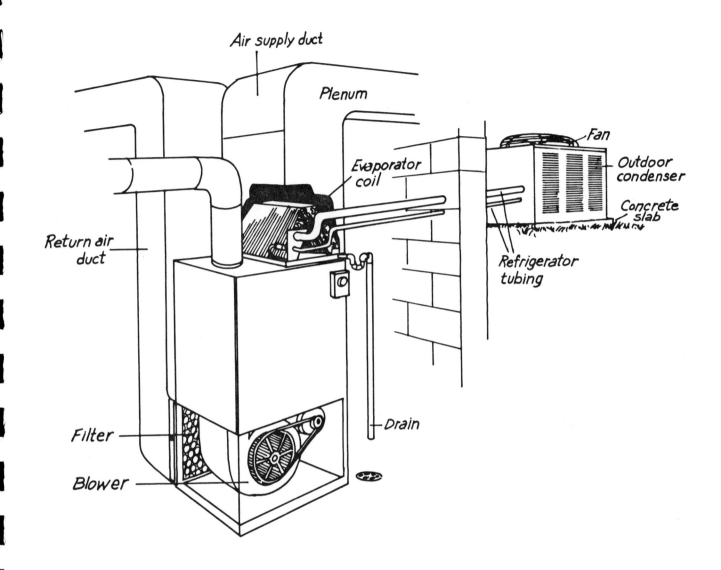

Air supply duct

Plenum

Evaporator coil

Fan

Outdoor condenser

Concrete slab

Return air duct

Refrigerator tubing

Filter

Blower

Drain

73

SECTION 4

Major Appliance Repairs

Refrigerator Troubleshooting

Tools: Long-handled brush, carpenter's level, wrench, refrigerator/freezer thermometer

If you are faced with a refrigerator malfunction, go through this basic troubleshooting chart before you call a service technician. Your problems might be as simple as a loose plug or clogged condenser coil. If these steps don't help, call for service because refrigerator systems are sealed at the factory and require specialized equipment and knowledge to repair. Remember, before you make any repair, turn the electricity off to the refrigerator.

Refrigerator does not run; interior light is out

Check the cord and plug. The plug may have been pulled loose from the power outlet, usually located behind the refrigerator. If the plug is hot, check the outlet (see pages 46–47) and the plug (see pages 50–51).

If pushing the plug tightly into the outlet does not get the refrigerator going, check the fuse or circuit breaker serving the refrigerator (see pages 38–39).

Refrigerator does not run; interior light works

If the interior light works, the refrigerator is getting power. To check the thermostat, turn it to a higher setting and listen for the compressor to start. Turn the thermostat off and on several times. If the compressor does not start, then the thermostat of the compressor is probably bad. Call a service technician.

If the compressor starts, run it for a minute or so and then stop to feel the plug, at the end of the cord where it is inserted into the wall receptacle. If it is hot, it is probably not making good contact with the outlet, thereby causing a low voltage situation. Clean or replace the plug or outlet. Remove all other appliances from the circuit and try to restart your refrigerator. If the same problem continues, call for a service technician.

Refrigerator is noisy

Check to see that the refrigerator is level, sitting squarely on the floor, but tilting slightly back so that its door closes on itself. Put a carpenter's level on top of the refrigerator and check for a horizontal straight line. If the refrigerator is not level, find the leveling legs in its bottom corners and adjust them by turning the legs clockwise with a wrench to raise the appliance and counterclockwise to lower it.

Refrigerator runs continually or is not cold enough

Check to see if the condenser is clogged with lint or dirt; if so, it cannot work effectively. This important part of your refrigerator condenses the refrigerant vapors back to liquid so it can be reused in the cooling process. As this happens, heat is discharged into the room.

You'll find condenser coils mounted on the back of some refrigerators or concealed behind the grille panel at the base of the refrigerator. Remove the bottom panel by gripping it at both sides and pulling it up and out. Use a long-handled brush or the crevice tool attachment of a vacuum cleaner to remove dirt and dust.

If the coils are clean and the problem persists, call a service technician.

Refrigerator temperature needs adjustment

Check your refrigerator's temperature. Set the thermostat so that food is kept at between 34–40° F. in the refrigerator compartment. Use a dial or liquid-filled refrigerator thermometer, available at hardware stores.

Food compartment test: Place the thermometer into a glass of water or container of food that has been in the refrigerator for at least twenty-four hours. Let the thermometer stand for three minutes and take a reading.

Freezer test: Insert the thermometer in a container of ice cream or between frozen food packages that have been in the freezer at least twenty-four hours. Wait three minutes; remove them and note the temperature. Place the thermometer in another part of the ice cream or between different frozen packages; after three minutes take another reading. Average the two temperatures. The ideal temperature for the freezer section is 0–4° F.

Adjust the temperature control knob higher or lower according to your findings.

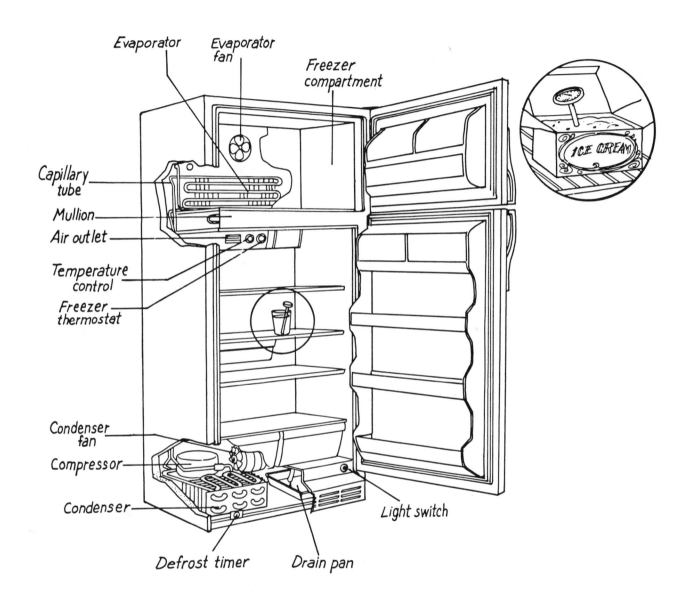

Evaporator

Evaporator fan

Freezer compartment

Capillary tube

Mullion

Air outlet

Temperature control

Freezer thermostat

Condenser fan

Compressor

Condenser

Defrost timer

Drain pan

Light switch

ICE CREAM

Dishwasher Troubleshooting

Tools: Adjustable wrench or screwdriver

Dishwashers are usually trouble-free, but when they do act up or leak there can be water everywhere. A broken water supply or drain hose can cause a flood in your kitchen. Before an emergency situation occurs, find and label the water shut-off valve for the dishwasher, which is located under the sink.

Other dishwasher problems are usually minor. These repairs are easy and of a general nature. Always consult your owner's manual for specific information and recommendations. Remember, before you make any repairs, turn off the water and electricity to the dishwasher.

Dishwasher overflows or leaks

A faulty timer, bad water valve solenoid or a stuck float switch can cause the dishwasher to overfill. This usually results in water leaking out the door seal. If water is leaking, turn off the water to the dishwasher. Don't open the dishwasher door. Allow the machine to complete the cycle and it will probably pump most of the water out.

Under normal operation the machine's timer should stop the water before the dishwasher overfills; if it doesn't, the float switch acts as a safety and shuts off the dishwasher. Check the action of the float switch; it should move up and down. Wiggle it up and down to loosen up any binding.

Remove as much water as possible. Clean the pump's screen and try the washer again, turning it on and then off. If the water stops, the valves are working. Turn the dishwasher on again and run it through a cycle. If it overflows, call a service technician (repairman).

Dishes do not come out clean

Poor washing performance is usually caused by food particles clogging the lower spray arm or pump. First, check the pump screen, located in the depression in the bottom of the dishwasher. Remove any food or particles so the water can flow freely into the pump located below the screen. The upper and lower arms are full of small holes that can be clogged by food particles. With a screw-driver or adjustable wrench, loosen the nut or screen on top of the arm; remove and clean it with an old tooth-brush to open all holes. See that the hot water heater thermostat is set either at 150° F. or the temperature suggested by the dishwasher manufacturer.

Dishwasher doesn't fill properly

If there isn't enough water in the dishwasher, you will not get proper dish cleaning. A timer opens the water inlet valve for a set period; if there is a clog in the water line or low water pressure, the dishwasher might not fully fill with water. Also, a faulty timer will close the water inlet valve early; a faulty valve will not open or may open only partially.

Check your water pressure and try using the dishwasher when other water-consuming fixtures (like the toilet, shower, and bathtub) will not be in use. If this does not help, call the repairman.

Water does not drain completely

A small amount of water will remain in the dishwasher. If more remains, check for a clogged pump screen (see above). Also check that the drain hose is not kinked or clogged and that the drain is running free.

Some installations have a device called an air gap, usually located on the counter near the back of the sink, to prevent back-siphoning of the drain water. Remove the decorative cover and check for accumulated grit that can obstruct air and water. Clean the air gap and replace the cover. If these measures don't cure the problem, call for a service technician.

Detergent remains in cup

First, look in your owner's manual to see if you are loading the soap dispenser properly. If there is old caked soap in the dispenser, scrape it out and wash the cup clean. Check that the cover moves freely; dried soap could be preventing it from opening. Always use fresh detergent intended specifically for an automatic dishwasher; old caked detergent will not wash dishes well.

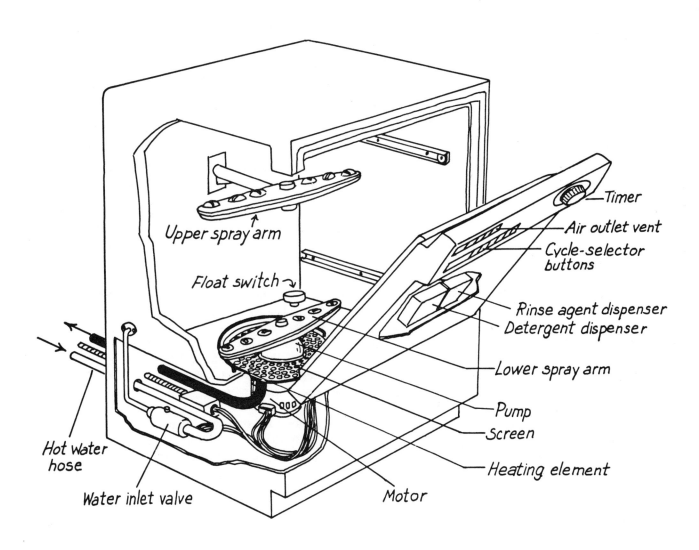

Upper spray arm

Float switch

Timer

Air outlet vent

Cycle-selector buttons

Rinse agent dispenser

Detergent dispenser

Lower spray arm

Pump

Screen

Heating element

Hot water hose

Water inlet valve

Motor

Clothes Washer Troubleshooting

Tools: Channel-lock pliers, adjustable wrench, carpenter's level

Clothes washers are reliable appliances and the single most important step you can take to keep them that way is to read and follow all instructions in the owner's manual. If you do experience problems, follow these simple repairs. They are of a general nature, but remember, always consult your owner's manual for specific information and recommendations. Remember to disconnect the washer's electrical cord from the outlet before making any repairs.

Machine overflows

Turn the timer dial to "off" to shut down the machine and stop the water flow. If the water keeps running, then the mixing valve is stuck open. Turn off the water supply to the machine at the shut-off valves, located on the wall or near the wash sink. To stop all water flow to the machine, turn these valves clockwise to close. If you cannot find the hot and cold valves, turn the water off at the main shut-off valve in your house (see pages 8–9).

Empty the machine by turning the timer dial to the spin cycle (and leave the water supply turned off). If the machine does not empty, then the pump or belt is bad and you should call a service technician. When the tub is empty, turn the machine off. Then turn the water back on; if water starts coming into the machine before you have turned it on, then the mixing valve is faulty. If the water doesn't start to flow until the timer dial is turned to a fill cycle, then the water-level switch is probably malfunctioning and you should call the repairman.

Try unsticking the mixing valve by turning the machine on and off several times with the timer dial. If this works, the repair is only temporary. Use the machine cautiously and watch it closely during the fill cycles because the valve might stick again. Call for a service technician to make a permanent repair.

Machine does not run

Check that the plug is securely plugged into a grounded outlet and that the fuse or circuit breaker in your home's electrical panel is working (see pages 38–

39). Next, check to see that the lid or door is properly closed. Some models have a switch on the lid that prevents the machine from running during the spin or other cycles when the top is opened; all front loading machines will not run with the door open. Also check the off-balance switch that shuts the machine down during the spin cycle if the basket vibrates wildly. If all of these seem normal, then you will have to call the repairman.

Machine is slow to fill with water or does not fill at all

Check to see that the water faucets leading into the machine are open. Also check to see that the water inlet hoses are not kinked and that the filters located in the ends of these hoses are free of clogs. Lint and dirt particles can obstruct the flow of water. To clean the hose filters, use a channel-lock pliers to loosen the hoses at the back of the machine. Remove the hoses and pry out the screens. Wash them clean and if they are badly corroded, purchase replacement screens at your local hardware store or home center.

Machine is noisy or vibrates

In the front at the bottom of the clothes washer are leveling feet that can be adjusted. Try to "rock" the machine back and forth to be sure it is resting firmly on the ground and all four leveling pads are in position. Place a carpenter's level on the machine's top; then use an adjustable wrench to turn the leveling feet until the washer no longer rocks. When filling the machine with heavy items, follow the manufacturer's suggestions on proper loading.

Object is stuck in agitator

First, make sure the machine is turned off. Reach into the machine and place both hands under the bottom of the agitator. With a sharp tug, lift the agitator up and off. Remove the object; then replace the agitator by reinserting it onto its shaft.

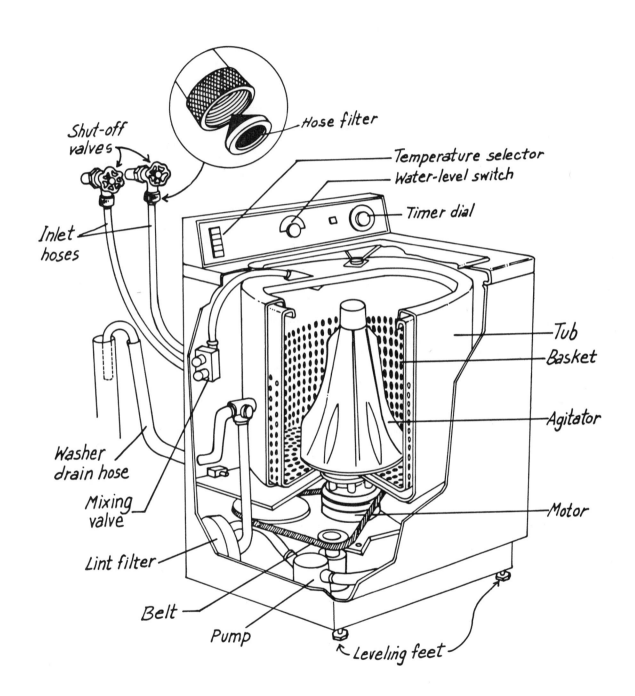

Shut-off valves

Hose filter

Temperature selector
Water-level switch

Timer dial

Inlet hoses

Tub

Basket

Agitator

Washer drain hose

Mixing valve

Lint filter

Motor

Belt

Pump

Leveling feet

81

Clothes Dryer Troubleshooting

Tools: Adjustable wrench, carpenter's level

Clothes dryers are very reliable. Most malfunctions can be traced to improper operation or overloading. The repairs described here are easy and of a general nature. Always consult your owner's manual for specific information and recommendations. Before you make any actual repair, turn the power off by disconnecting the dryer's electrical cord from the outlet or at your home's main electrical panel.

Dryer does not turn on

Whether you have a gas or an electric machine, first check to see that its power cord is plugged in and that the fuse or circuit breaker in your house's main electrical panel is operating properly (see pages 38–39). Also check to see that the clothes dryer's door is firmly closed.

If the dryer still does not run, turn the dryer's power off, open its door, and look for the door switch, located on the edge of the door frame. The switch lever should move freely and be pushed completely in when the door is closed. Work the switch lever to see that it moves easily; then close the door and try the machine again. If your dryer has power and the door switch is operative, but the dryer does not work, call a service technician.

Dryer runs but does not dry clothes sufficiently

Clean the lint trap and check the exhaust vent system.

Clogging can be caused by an accumulation of lint and dust.

If you have a gas clothes dryer, the pilot light may be out. To relight the pilot, consult your owner's manual. Here are some general instructions. Remove the lower access panel and read the directions printed on the inside of the panel for relighting the pilot. The procedure is simple—push a reset button down while holding a match to the pilot. Keep the reset button depressed for about 30 seconds until the pilot flame heats the safety thermocouple; then release the button. The pilot should remain lit; if it goes out, repeat the lighting process. Wooden or long fireplace matches should be used to light the pilot.

Dryer runs noisily

A loose object in the drum is the major cause of noise. Check inside the dryer for coins, buttons or other loose hard objects.

If the dryer is noisy and vibrates, check to see if the machine rocks back and forth on its leveling feet. To check for levelness, turn the dryer off and unplug it. With a wrench, adjust the four leveling feet in each corner of the base of the dryer; turn them clockwise to be lowered, counterclockwise to be raised. Place a carpenter's level on the dryer's top; then use an adjustable wrench to turn the feet until the machine is level and does not rock.

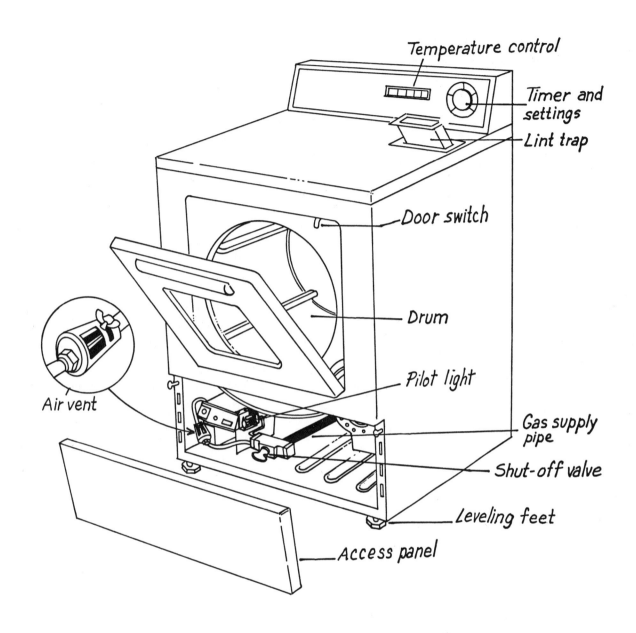

Temperature control

Timer and settings

Lint trap

Door switch

Drum

Pilot light

Gas supply pipe

Shut-off valve

Leveling feet

Air vent

Access panel

83

Garbage Disposal Troubleshooting

Tools: Kitchen tongs or pliers

Garbage disposals usually digest just about anything you can put down them but sometimes they do act up. Always follow the suggestions in your owner's manual. If the disposal does not work, try these simple repairs, which are general in nature. Always consult your owner's manual for specific information and recommendations. Before a repair that entails unclogging your garbage disposal, turn the electricity off at the machine's switch or at your home's main electrical panel.

Disposal makes no noise and does not work

First, check that the garbage disposal is able to get power. The plug should be securely in the outlet and the appropriate circuit breaker or fuse should be working (see pages 38–39). Look for the overload breaker reset button (it's usually red) on the garbage disposal motor. Push the reset button in until you feel or hear a click. If, after you have checked the power supply and reset the overload button, your machine still doesn't work and you don't hear the motor hum when you turn it on, call a service technician.

Disposal is jammed and will not operate

If the disposal hums but does not work, it is probably jammed. Check your owner's manual to see if your unit has a switch that allows the motor to reverse and free itself. If you don't have a manual or that type of unit, turn the power switch off and turn off the power to its circuit breaker or fuse box.

Shine a flashlight down the garbage disposal's drain to see if you can discover what is causing the jam. Use a piece of wood, like a broom or mop handle, to try to force the cutting blades loose (see facing illustration). Push the wood against the sharp side of the blade and try to force the blades away from the jam. If you have silverware stuck inside, use kitchen tongs or pliers to pull it out. *Never put your hand inside the disposal!*

When the jam-up is freed, turn the power back on, push the red reset button, and turn the garbage disposal back on. Run water through it to remove any residue Call a repairman if the problem still isn't resolved.

Power switch

Reset button

Gas Range Troubleshooting

Tools: Screwdriver

A gas appliance, especially a kitchen range, is very dependable. Most problems with a stove are caused by dirty burners and pilot lights. If after you complete these basic repairs the range continues to work improperly, call a service technician. If you can smell gas before or after you work on the range, you have a gas leak. This can be serious; call the gas company immediately!

Stove-top burner does not light

Sometimes food particles or dirt accumulates in the tip of the pilot light and closes it off. This problem is easy to fix. Remove the range top to expose the pilot lights. Turn all stove controls "off." Then remove the small cap or cover on the pilot lights and clean away any residue. Clear the gas opening in the pilot light by poking a straight pin into the small gas hole. Scrub the tubes leading from the burners to the pilot with a strong detergent and a stiff brush. Hold a lit match over the gas hole in the pilot light and the pilot should light. If it does not, check to make sure that the gas supply to the stove is on.

If the pilot flame is not steady and at least 1/8" above the pilot light shield, it should be adjusted. Trace the gas supply line running to the pilot light back to the front of the stove. Where the tube joins the other valves, you probably will see an adjustment screw. Use a screwdriver to turn it counterclockwise to increase the pilot light size. If after relighting the pilot light, the burners do not work, call your gas company.

Stove-top burner does not light with electronic ignition

Most modern ranges have electronic ignition, recognizable by a clicking sound when you turn the burner on. If you hear the click, but the burner does not light, you could have a dirty pilot light electrode (a small pointed metal rod between the tubes that lead to the burners).

Clean these electrodes, but first unplug the range. Use a small brush to clean away anything blocking the igniter. To reach it you may have to remove the metal bridge or cover over the electrode. After you have cleaned the pilot electrodes but they don't spark and light the burners, call a service technician.

Oven burner does not light

The oven pilot light is usually located in the back of the oven. You can see it if you open the broiler compartment. If it has gone out, clean and relight it by following the steps outlined above for the stove-top burner pilot. Use a long wooden match to relight the oven pilot.

Oven light or control panel light goes out

Remove the light bulb from the oven and replace it with an appliance bulb.

To remove the light in the oven's control panel, first unplug the range. Then refer to your owner's manual to disassemble the panel covering the light. Usually screws along the sides of the panel hold it in place. Remove the defective light bulb and buy an exact replacement.

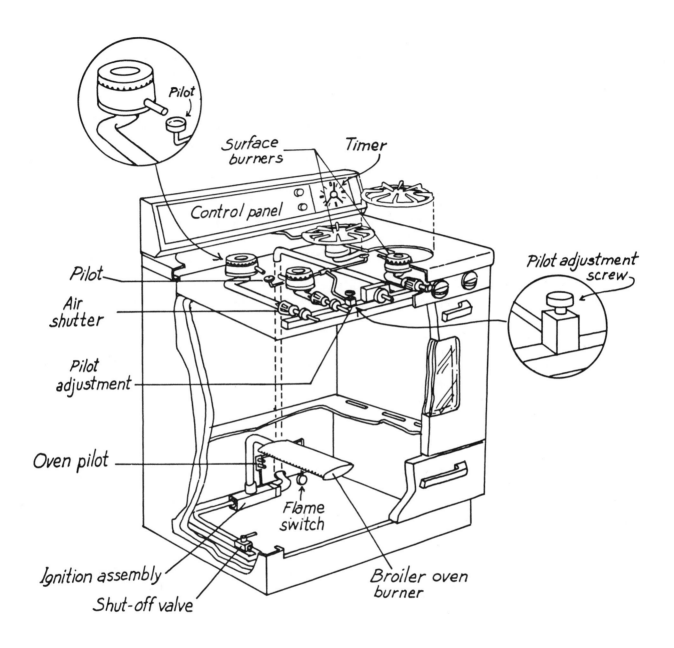

Pilot

Surface burners

Timer

Control panel

Pilot

Air shutter

Pilot adjustment

Pilot adjustment screw

Oven pilot

Flame switch

Ignition assembly

Shut-off valve

Broiler oven burner

87

Electric Range Troubleshooting

Tools: Screwdriver

Electric ranges are easy to service. With little difficulty the heating elements can be removed and replaced.

Range will not heat

Check that the fuses or circuit breakers serving the stove are not blown or open. The stove is on a 220-volt circuit and has two cartridge fuses or two circuit breakers serving it (see pages 38–39).

Stove-top element does not heat

Before you check the heating element, turn off the power to the range at the service panel. Your range has either plug-in heating elements or elements that are attached to the stove by easy-to-remove wires. Refer to your owner's manual for specific replacement instructions. Remove the defective element and take it with you when buying a replacement at a repair facility that carries your brand of appliance.

Oven heating element does not work

Before you check the heating element, turn off the power to the range at the service panel. The oven heating element is removable; refer to your owner's manual for specific replacement information. Remove the defective element and take it with you when you buy a replacement at a repair facility carrying your brand of appliance.

Oven light or control panel light is out

Remove the light bulb from the oven and buy an appliance replacement bulb.

To remove the light in the control panel, first unplug the range. Then refer to your owner's manual for how to disassemble the panel covering the light. Usually, screws at either end and along the top of the panel hold it in place. Remove the defective light bulb and buy an exact replacement.

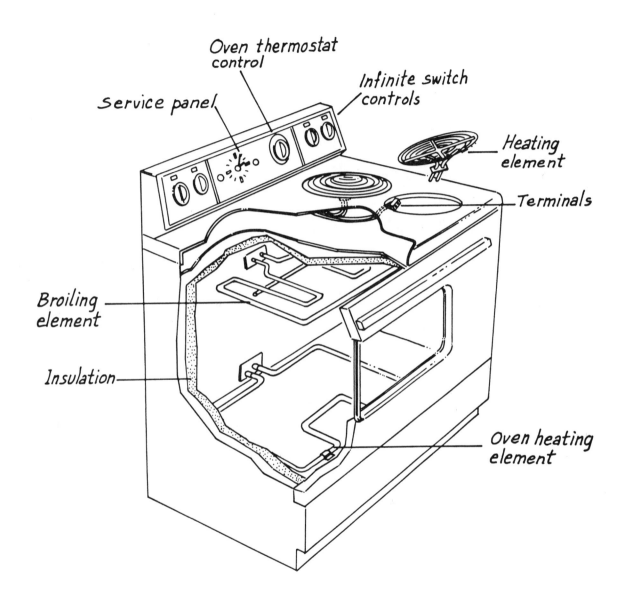

Oven thermostat control

Infinite switch controls

Service panel

Heating element

Terminals

Broiling element

Insulation

Oven heating element

89

Repair or Replace Major Appliances?

In general, if the cost of the repair is 50 percent of the cost of a new appliance or more, it is time to buy a new one. The chart below shows the average lifespan for various appliances.

Always choose an authorized service center when having an appliance repaired so you're certain the repair person is properly trained and uses the right replacement parts. If the appliance is under warranty, do not attempt to fix it yourself because that can void the warranty.

The average life of major household appliances

Freezer	20 years
Refrigerator	15 years
Gas Range	12–15 years
Air Conditioner	12–15 years
Clothes Dryer (gas)	13 years
Clothes Dryer (electric)	11–13 years
Electric Range	12 years
Clothes Washer	11 years
Dishwasher	11 years

SECTION 5

Interior Wall and Ceiling Repairs

Repair Popped Drywall Nail

Tools: Hammer, nail set, putty knife with 3″ flexible blade, sanding block

If your house is less than thirty years old, it probably has walls and ceilings made of gypsum board. The gypsum board or drywall is held to the studs by nails. Sometimes one works loose or "pops" when the studs dry out and warp or shrink. The loose "popped" nail then protrudes from the drywall, causing a round or crescent crack in the drywall compound hiding the head. As long as the nail is loose in the wall, the crack will come back no matter how many times you apply Spackle over it.

1) Secure the nail

A popped nail can be secured in two ways: Pull the nail out of the wall with a claw hammer; or if you can't get at the nail head, use a hammer and a nail set to drive the drywall nail into the wall tight against the stud. (*Illustration A.*)

2) Install new nail

Place a new drywall nail a couple of inches above the original. With a hammer, drive the new nail straight into the drywall and, to hide the nail head, make a slight dimple in the surrounding surface with the last hammer blow. (*Illustration B.*)

3) Fill old nail hole with Spackle

Use a putty knife with a flexible 3″-wide blade to apply a premixed wall patching compound called Spackle. (*Illustration C.*) Fill the hole left by the popped nail and the dimple around the new nail head with Spackle.

4) Sand smooth and prime for painting

When dry, sand the area smooth (*Illustration D*) and apply a second thin coat of Spackle. Feather (spread thinly) the Spackle several inches beyond the edges of the patch. This thin coat dries in several hours depending on humidity. Sand the repair with a medium-grade sandpaper. To make sanding easier, wrap the sandpaper around a small block of wood or purchase a sanding block at your local hardware store. Prepare the patched area for painting by applying an interior latex wall primer paint before painting or wallpapering.

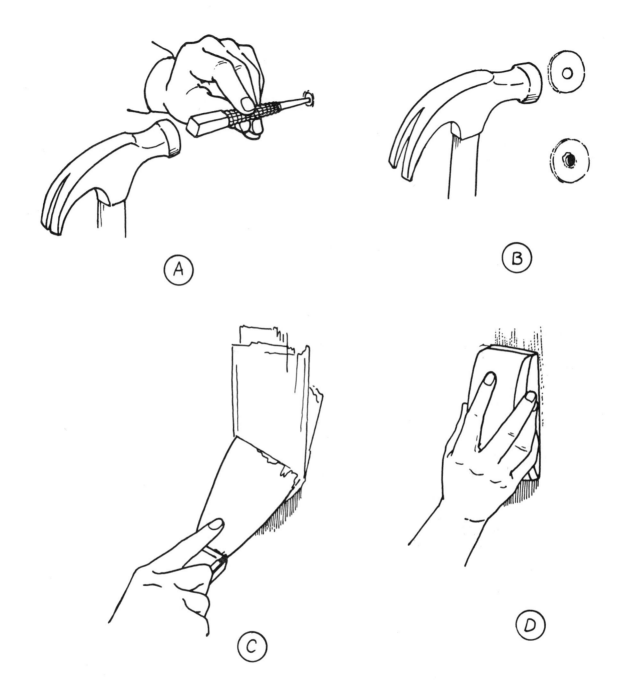

Patch a Gouge or Small Hole in Drywall

Tools: Hammer, putty knife with 3–5″ flexible blade, sanding block, utility knife

To repair a surface gouge in gypsum-board drywall, use a putty knife with a wide flexible blade and Spackle. To repair a small hole in drywall, use the same tools as for a popped nail (see page 92), but instead of Spackle, use fast-setting patching plaster. As mentioned below, a piece of cardboard with a knotted string in its center will prevent the patching plaster from falling through the hole into the cavity behind the wall.

TO PATCH SURFACE GOUGE

1) Level area around repair

Push the putty knife blade over the gouge or nail hole. (*Illustration A.*) The blade will hesitate or "hang up" at the high spots, so make them level.

2) Fill cracks; then sand, prime, and paint

Apply Spackle to fill the gouge with a putty knife. (*Illustration B.*) Make a final pass over the repair with the putty knife blade held at a 45-degree angle to smooth the Spackle level with the wall face. When the Spackle is dry, sand smooth and apply a second thin coat. Feather (spread thinly) the Spackle several inches beyond the edges of the patch. When the area is dry, sand it smooth with a medium-grade sandpaper wrapped around a wood block or with a sanding block. Before you repaint the patch, apply a coat of interior latex wall primer paint.

TO PATCH SMALL HOLE

1) Use cardboard to hold plaster in hole

Take a small piece of cardboard and pull a piece of string with a knot at its end through the center of the cardboard. (*Illustration C.*) Fold the cardboard in half and push it through the drywall hole. (*Illustration D.*) Then pull the string taut to hold the cardboard against the inside of the wall. Apply patching plaster to the hole with a putty knife. Make sure that the plaster goes behind the wallboard. Fill the hole with patching plaster until it is about 1/8″ below the wall surface.

2) Cut string, then topcoat with Spackle

In 3–5 minutes or when the plaster begins to set, you can release the string. After the plaster has hardened, cut the string with a utility knife. (*Illustration E.*) Score the patch's surface with the edge of the putty knife. Apply a topcoat of premixed Spackle. When the area is dry, apply a second thin coat of Spackle, feathering it beyond the edge of the repair. Before repainting, sand the patch and apply a coat of interior latex wall primer paint.

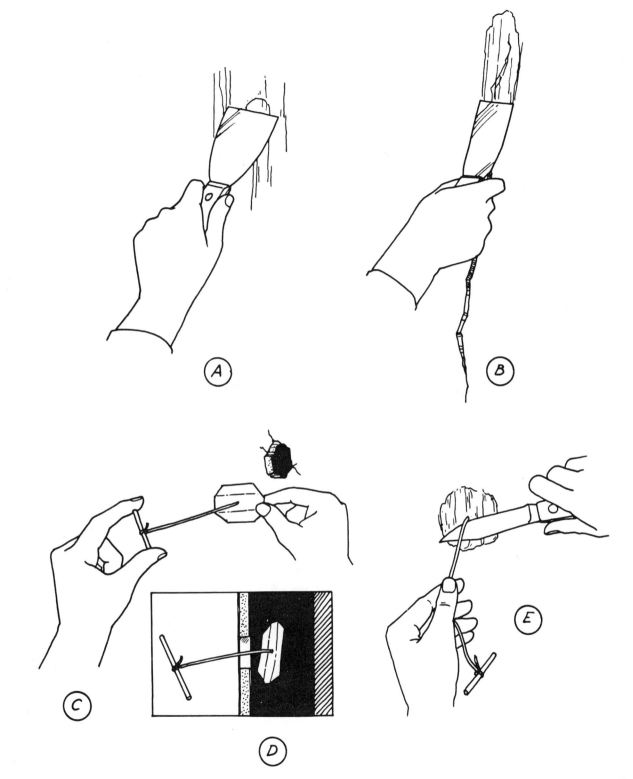

A

B

C

D

E

95

Patch Cracks in Plaster

Tools: Putty knife with 1½" stiff blade, putty knife with 3–5" flexible blade, ¾" cold chisel or old wood chisel, sanding block, old paint brush

If your house is over thirty years old you most likely have plaster walls. Through the years most plaster walls develop small cracks over doors, around windows, and in other stress areas. Repairing these cracks is not difficult and should be done before painting.

1) Open cracks into shallow V

Use a putty knife with a 1½" stiff blade, a screwdriver, or the point of a beverage can opener to open the small cracks into a shallow V. (*Illustration A.*) Remove any dust or loose plaster with an old paintbrush or hairbrush.

2) Moisten crack and surrounding area

To prevent the dry plaster from absorbing the water from the Spackle (mentioned below) before it has time to properly set, moisten the edges of the cracks with water.

Use a spray bottle (*Illustration B*) or damp rag.

3) Apply Spackle compound

Spread premixed spackling compound into the cracks with a flexible bladed 3–5" putty knife. (*Illustration C.*) Hold the blade at a 45-degree angle to the surface, forcing the compound well into the cracks. Remove excess Spackle by dragging the blade across the patch.

4) Topcoat with Spackle, then sand and prime

Let the patch dry, then apply a second coat of Spackle. Sand the area lightly with a medium-grade sandpaper wrapped around a wood block, or else with a sanding block. (*Illustration D.*) Apply an interior latex primer prior to painting or wallpapering.

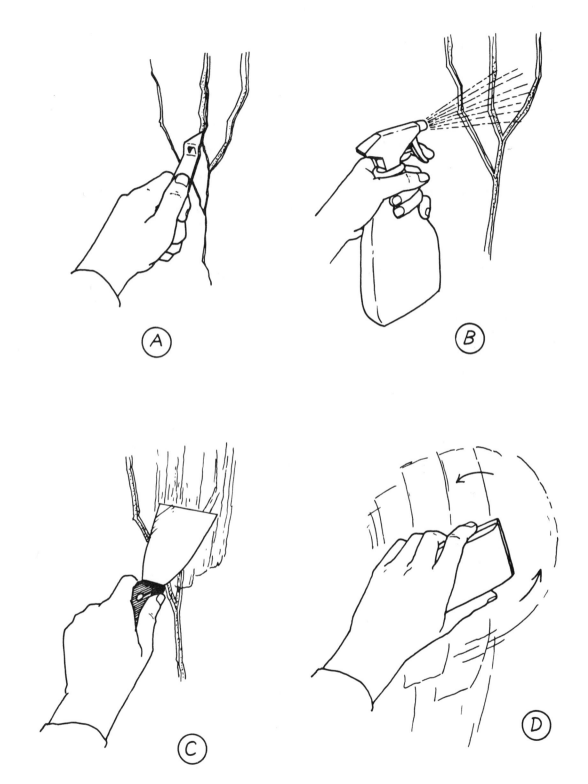

Patch Holes in Plaster

Tools: Hammer, 3/4" cold chisel or old wood chisel, putty knife with 1½" stiff blade, putty knife with 3–5" flexible blade, sanding block

Sometimes large cracks or holes develop in old walls. Leave the repair of a gaping hole to a plasterer, but you should be able to repair large cracks and small holes in your plaster walls. The most important point to remember is to remove all the loose plaster from the area you are patching because the patch will crack when it comes in contact with any old loose plaster.

1) Remove old plaster

Remove any loose chunks of plaster with a hammer. Use a cold chisel (chisel with all-metal handle) or an old woodworking chisel to remove the stubborn pieces of plaster. (*Illustration A.*) Undercut the edges of the hole with the chisel (*see the inset illustration*) to provide a good bond between the patch and old plaster. Remove any plaster dust with an old paintbrush or hairbrush.

2) Repair lath

Remove any broken lath (the wood strips nailed to studs that the plaster is attached to). If the lath is loose, use a hammer to renail it to the studs with drywall nails. (*Illustration B.*) If the lath is not repairable and the hole is small, use the cardboard-and-string remedy for repairing drywall (see pages 94–95).

3) Wet area, then apply plaster

Moisten the rough edges of the hole and lath with water. Use a spray bottle, wet rag or sponge. (*Illustration C.*) Mix the patching plaster with water, following the manufacturer's directions. Apply the first coat of the plaster with a stiff-bladed putty knife. Fill the crack or hole with plaster to about 1/8" below the wall surface. When the patching plaster has set, scratch the surface of the patch with the edge of the putty knife. Mix up another batch of patching plaster and apply a second coat, leveling it with the wall surface.

4) Topcoat with Spackle, then sand

After the plaster is dry, use a putty knife with a wide flexible blade to apply a third and final topcoat of premixed Spackle. (*Illustration D.*) Feather (spread thinly) this coat several inches beyond the edge of the patch. When the area is dry, sand smooth with a medium-grade sandpaper wrapped around a wood block, or with a sanding block. Apply an interior latex primer prior to painting or wallpapering.

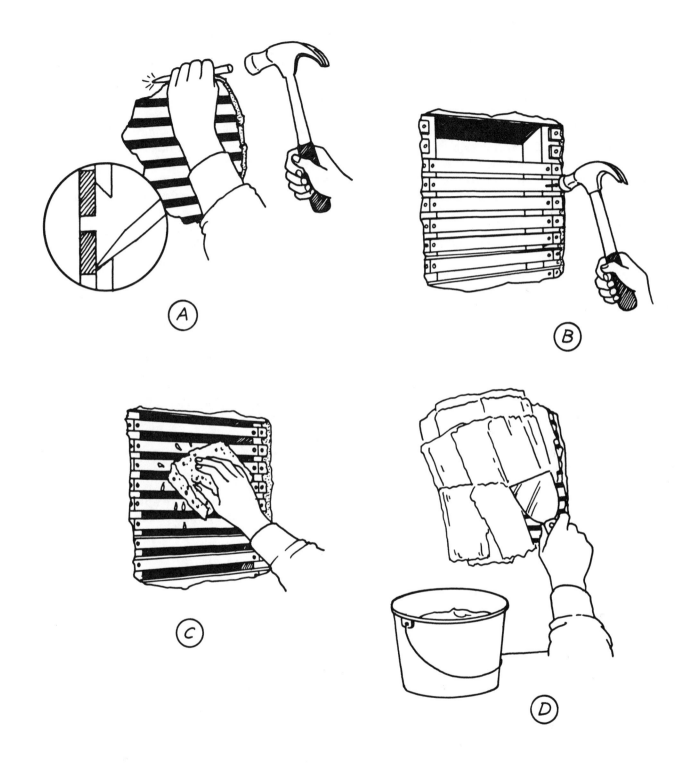

Replace a Loose or Damaged Ceramic Tile

Tools: Hammer, cold chisel or nail set, screwdriver, glass cutter, pliers, file

Ceramic tile is very durable but it can be damaged or come loose from the wall. Don't put off making this repair because water can get behind the damaged or loose tile and eventually destroy your entire wall.

1) Remove broken tile

If the tile is cracked but still tight in the wall, remove it by striking its center with a hammer and the point of a small cold chisel or nail set. (*Illustration A.*) This will break the tile and you can remove the pieces. If the tile is good, but loose, use a small chisel or old screwdriver to remove the old grout (plaster) that holds the damaged tile in place. Work carefully so as not to damage the surrounding tiles. After the tile is out, scrape away all old grout and remove as much of the old tile's adhesive caulk as possible.

Take the old tile or a piece of it to your local tile outlet and purchase a close match. While you're there, buy a small amount of tile adhesive and grout.

2) Score tile with glass cutter

If the bad tile is cut to fit around a fixture, you can cut a replacement. First, draw a line with a pencil, before using a glass cutter to score the outline of the shape you want. Then score lines across the area of the tile you want to discard. (*Illustration B.*)

3) Nip tile to shape with pliers

Carefully break off small pieces of tile from the waste area with a pliers or tile nippers. (*Illustration C.*) Then use a file to smooth the edges of the tile.

Put the tile in place and check that it lies flush with the other tiles. If it protrudes, remove more of the old adhesive from the wall. Also check that pieces of the old grout are not behind the tile.

4) Apply adhesive to tile

Apply a small amount of tile adhesive or adhesive caulk to the center of the tile back. (*Illustration D.*) Keep the adhesive away from the edges or it will push out between the tiles. Gently push the tile in place, rocking it back and forth to spread the adhesive.

5) Mix grout and work into joints

Mix a small amount of tile grout with water, following the manufacturer's directions. Dampen all joints to be grouted with water. Fill these joints with grouting cement, working it into all crevices with your fingers. Force the grout deeply into the joints by pushing the end of an old toothbrush handle or a craft stick over them. (*Illustration E.*)

6) Remove excess grout with sponge

Apply more grout if there are spaces or voids around the tile. Allow the grout to set for 10–15 minutes; then remove any excess from the tile faces with a sponge and water. (*Illustration F.*)

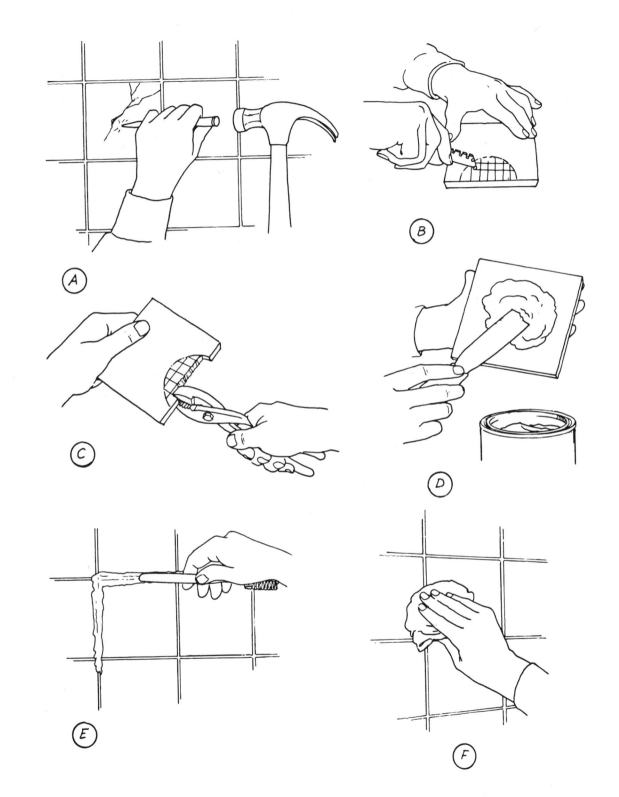

Remove Old Wallpaper from Walls

Tools and Materials: 1"-wide masking tape, plastic drop cloths, garden sprayer, wallpaper scraper or putty knife with 6" flexible blade, sponge, trisodium phosphate (TSP)

Removing old wallpaper isn't difficult but it can be messy. Here is an easy way to soak the paper off and contain the mess. First, prepare the room by placing all furniture and wall decorations in the center and covering them with drop cloths. Remove any electrical switch plate covers and light fixtures. Turn off the electricity in the room.

1) Apply masking tape to baseboard

Protect your floor with 1" or wider masking tape and plastic drop cloths. Attach one edge of the tape to the top of the baseboard molding (*Illustration A*), leaving the other tape edge free to stick to one edge of the drop cloth.

2) Attach drop cloth to baseboard tape

Partially unfold the drop cloth and stretch it along the wall you taped. (*Illustration B.*) Lift the free edge of the tape and stick the drop cloth to it; then unfold the drop cloth into the room.

3) Soak walls with remover solution

Pour hot water and wallpaper remover solution into a garden sprayer according to manufacturer's mixing directions. (*Illustration C.*) You should plan to work on a 6'-wide section of the wall at one time. Use a flexible bladed scraper or putty knife to score the wallpaper in several areas so that the solution can get behind the paper to soak it thoroughly. Soak the wallpaper with the solution in your garden sprayer, beginning at the top of the wall. Apply as much solution as the paper will absorb; wait until it soaks in, then resoak. Let the solution do the work; it will take approximately 20 minutes or so, depending on the number of layers of paper. Several light soakings are more effective than one heavy one. Prepare another section of the wall while the first area is soaking.

4) When glue is soft, scrape off wallpaper

After the glue from the solution begins to soften, peel the wallpaper off with a broad knife scraper and discard the paper onto the drop cloth. (*Illustration D.*) If you are working on drywall, use a putty knife. Be careful not to damage the drywall's paper face. Several layers of wallpaper might require resoaking.

5) Wash glue from wall, then remove drop cloth

While the wall remains moist, use a sponge and a solution of trisodium phosphate (TSP) and water to remove any excess wallpaper and paste. When finished, remove the tape and drop cloth from the baseboards. Wrap the wallpaper droppings in the drop cloth and discard. (*Illustration E.*)

Replace a Loose or Damaged Ceiling Tile

Tools: Utility knife, pliers, putty knife, paint roller

Acoustical ceiling tiles are easily damaged, especially in a basement recreation room where clearance is low. These tiles will also stain if they get wet. Here's how to replace them.

1) Remove tile from grid

The tiles in a suspended ceiling can easily be taken down and replaced. If your ceiling has a visible grid and the tiles can be pushed up, then all you have to do is remove the tile with a sharp utility knife and purchase a replacement tile.

Many older ceilings are glued or stapled in place and repairing a single tile is a little more involved. If the tiles are only stained, correct the cause of the stain first, then paint the tiles with shellac to seal the stain. Use a heavy-napped roller to paint the entire ceiling with latex paint.

2) Cut through joints to free tile

If a tile is damaged, remove it with a sharp knife by cutting through the joint between it and the surrounding tiles. (*Illustration A.*) If it's stubborn, cut it into several pieces and remove each piece individually. Be careful not to damage adjoining tiles.

3) Clean glue or staples from ceiling

Use a pair of pliers to remove nails or staples from the surrounding framing. (*Illustration B.*) Scrape off any glue and clean away any dust or ceiling material.

4) Cut tongue from replacement tiles

You cannot slip a new tile in place because of its interlocking tongue. Place the new tile on a clean, flat surface and cut the tongue edges away with a utility knife. (*Illustration C.*) The tile will then fit. If you have several tiles to replace, you can slip all but the last one into place without cutting off the tongues.

5) Apply mastic and push tile in place

Use a putty knife to apply mastic or adhesive to the back of the new tile. (*Illustration D.*) Then insert it into the ceiling opening. Hold the tile in place carefully, pushing it level with surrounding tiles, until the adhesive sets.

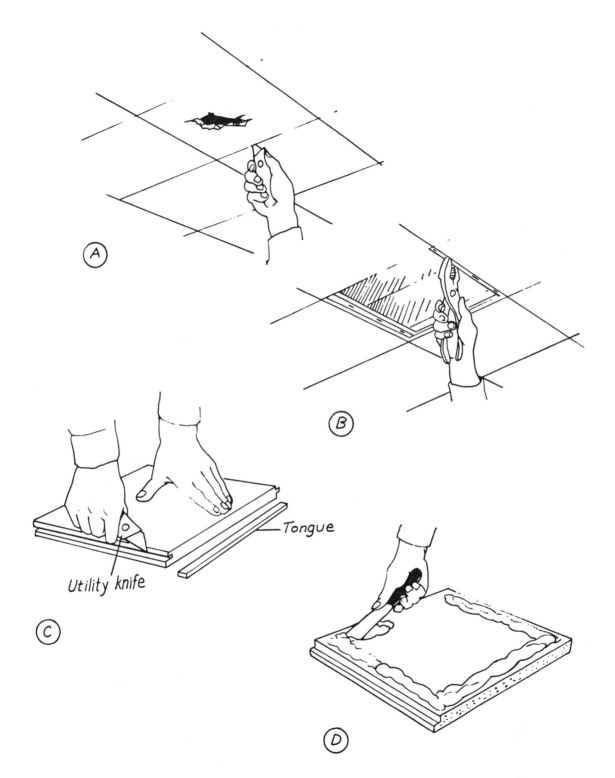

Tongue

Utility knife

A

B

C

D

SECTION 6

Floor and Stair Repairs

Fix a Squeaky Floor

Tools: Hammer, drill, 3/16″ and 1/4″ drill bits, screwdriver, nail set

Is there anything more annoying than a squeaky floor? The culprit is usually in the subfloor and can be corrected at floor level or from a basement or crawl space. This is a two-person repair project because it needs someone moving around in the squeaky floor area and another person in the basement or crawl space listening for the source of the squeak. Following are several suggested remedies for this problem.

1) Make repairs from floor's underside

If you can get at the underside of your floor from the basement or crawl space, look for a gap between the floorboards (actually the subfloor) and the floor joists, in the area of the squeak. A common cause of squeaks is when the subfloor rubs against the floor joist or a nail as someone walks over the area. An easy way to fix this is to apply carpenter's glue to a small wedge of wood and, with a hammer, drive the wood shingle tightly between the subfloor and joist. (*Illustration A.*) Wood shingles and carpenter's glue are sold at your local lumberyard.

2) Pull floor together with screws from below

Another solution is to drive several 1 1/4″-long #10 flathead wood screws into the floor from below. The screws pull the floorboards together and stop the squeak. Drill a 3/16″-wide pilot hole through the subfloor (the flooring you can see from the basement) and into the hardwood flooring. Wrap a piece of masking tape around the drill bit, 1 1/4″ from its end, so you can see how deep you are drilling. Then drill a 1/4″ diameter hole through the subfloor only. The larger hole in the subfloor allows the screw to pull the hardwood and subfloor together. Put a little soap on the screw threads to make it easier to turn the screw into the hardwood flooring. Next, insert the screws and tighten them with a screwdriver. (*Illustration B.*) Have your helper stand on the floor above while you give the screws a final tightening.

3) Angle nails through loose flooring from above

If you cannot get at the underside of your floor, pinpoint the squeak and, through the flooring, drill small pilot holes for annular ringed flooring nails.

Purchase a small box of these nails at your local hardware store or home center. If they don't have this type of nail, purchase #6d galvanized finish or casing nails. These have rough shanks and hold in place well. Drill a 1/16″-wide diameter pilot hole through the flooring into joists or between joists into the subflooring. Angle these holes for the greatest holding power. Drive the nails into these pilot holes (*Illustration C*), then use a nail set to sink the nail heads below the surface and fill in all holes with wood filler.

The nails stop the floorboards from moving and squeaking. A quick temporary fix for a minor squeak is to sprinkle a dry lubricant, such as liquid wax, powdered soap, graphite or talcum powder, between the squeaky boards.

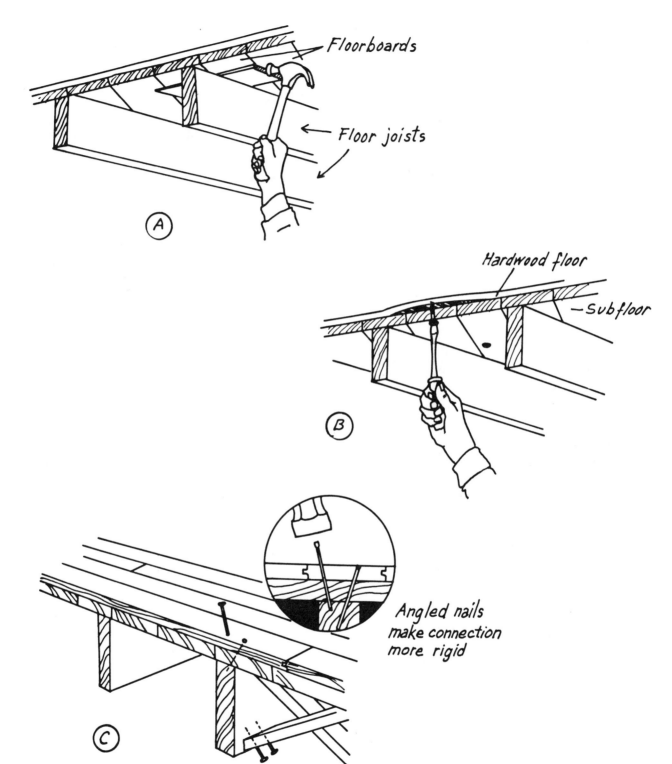

Floorboards

Floor joists

A

Hardwood floor

Subfloor

B

Angled nails
make connection
more rigid

C

109

Fix a Squeaky Stair

Tools: Drill, 1/16″ drill bit, hammer, nail set, putty knife, utility knife

Squeaky stairs are often an annoyance. You should be aware that in many cases finding the squeak and silencing it are not difficult to do. Several ways this repair can be made are described below.

1) Locate area of squeak

Most squeaks come from the rubbing of the stair tread (the board you step on) against the riser (the back of the stair) and the stringers (the sides of the stair).

2) Use nails to stop squeak at front of stair tread

If you can't get behind your stairs and the squeak seems to come from the joint between the tread and the riser, use finishing nails driven through the tread into the riser. Drill 1/16″ pilot holes through the tread into the top edge of the riser. Angle the holes for better holding. Next, drive 6d finishing nails through these holes. (*Illustration A.*) Then, with a hammer and nail set, sink the nail heads below the surface of the tread. Use a putty knife to spread wood filler into all holes.

3) Use wedge to stop squeak at back of stair tread

If you can't get behind the stair and the squeak seems to come from the back of the tread, get some small wood wedges and carpenter's glue from your local lumberyard. Wet the pointed end of the wedge with glue and, with a hammer and a small wood driving block, drive it into the joint between the back of the tread and the riser. (*Illustration B.*) After you have three or four wedges in place, cut them flush with the face of the riser, with a sharp utility knife. (*Illustration C.*) Clean up any excess glue with a wet rag before it has a chance to dry.

4) Glue blocks to back of treads and risers

If you can get behind the stairs, a more permanent repair can be made by using carpenter's glue to glue blocks of wood to the underside of the treads and back of the risers. Then use 4d nails or 1 1/4″ #8 wood screws to hold the blocks in place. (*Illustration D.*) You can also drive wooden wedges into the joint (*Illustration E*) using the same technique as described in Step #3 above.

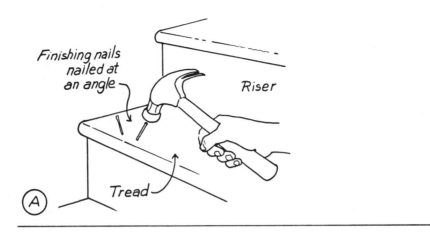

Finishing nails nailed at an angle

Riser

Tread

(A)

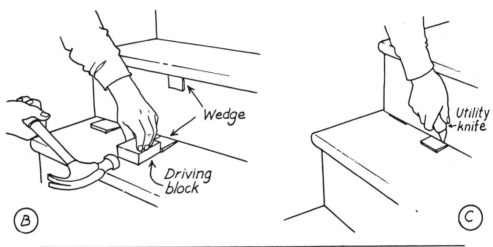

Wedge

Driving block

(B)

Utility knife

(C)

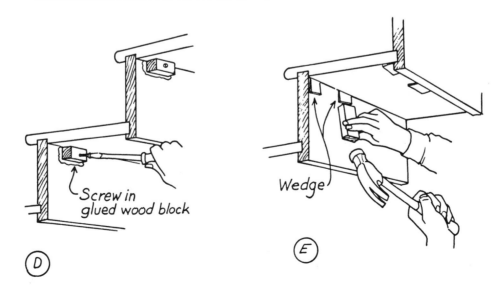

Screw in glued wood block

(D)

Wedge

(E)

111

Replace Baseboard Molding

Tools: Pry bar, hammer, screwdriver, saw, nail set

The wooden baseboard at the bottom of a wall is there to protect the wall surface from damage and to conceal the gap where the floor meets the wall. You have to remove the baseboard from the wall to repair or replace it if it becomes marred or dented.

1) Remove damaged base shoe and baseboard section

Begin by removing the damaged baseboard section with a pry bar and hammer. Remove the base shoe (small molding next to floor) by inserting the thin end of the pry bar between the baseboard and shoe and gently prying outward. (*Illustration A.*) If it is a long run of base shoe, insert a screwdriver in the gap between the baseboard and base shoe as you work along the wall until you can easily pull the whole base shoe loose. Work a short section at a time; if you pull at the end of the base shoe, the leverage you exert can break the molding in the center or at the other end. Remove the baseboard from the wall in the same manner.

2) Remove old nails from wall

Remove any remaining nails with a hammer. Put a piece of wood between the hammerhead and wall to prevent damage to the plaster or wallboard. (*Illustration B.*)

3) Use old piece of molding as pattern

Use the damaged piece of molding as a pattern to cut a replacement piece. (*Illustration C.*) You can also salvage the good part of the old molding. With a saw, cut off the damaged section at a 45-degree angle. Cut a matching angle on the end of the new piece and copy the angle or contour of the old molding.

4) Use new nails to install molding

Position the replacement piece of molding and hammer it in place using #6d finishing nails. First, drill pilot holes for the nails, close to the molding end. Install the old base shoe in the same manner or purchase a new base shoe. Drive in the nailheads with a nail set. (*Illustration D.*) Fill holes with wood filler, and paint or stain to match the previous molding.

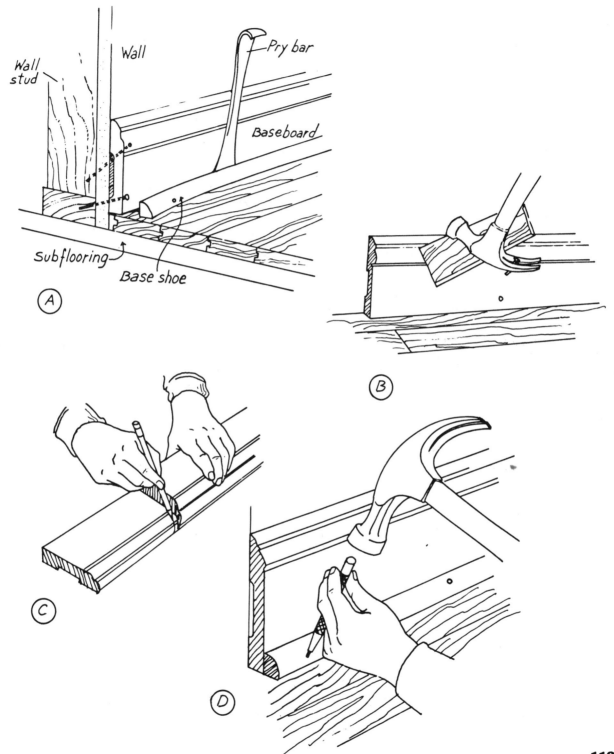

Wall stud

Wall

Pry bar

Baseboard

Subflooring

Base shoe

A

B

C

D

Replace Floor Tile

Tools: Clothes iron, putty knife or hammer and chisel, utility knife, notched trowel

The best way to repair a damaged tile is to replace it with a new one. The repair is an easy one; the challenge is not to damage the surrounding tiles while you remove the bad one.

1) Heat old tile to remove it

Use a clothes iron set at low heat to soften the floor adhesive under the damaged tile. Move the iron slowly across the tile. (*Illustration A.*) Avoid scorching other tiles that surround the repair by covering them with aluminum foil.

2) Carefully pry up old tile

When the adhesive is soft, use a putty knife to pry the tile up. (*Illustration B.*) Work from the center of the damaged tile to avoid damage to the edges of the surrounding tiles, first using a utility knife to make a cut in the center of the bad tile. If it is stubborn, use a hammer and chisel.

3) Scrape away old glue and level area

Remove the tile and with a putty knife scrape away the old adhesive, creating a smooth surface for the new tile to rest on. (*Illustration C.*) Check to see that the new tile will fit perfectly. If it's too large, sand it down to size by rubbing its edges with sandpaper.

4) Spread mastic and replace tile

Spread mastic (adhesive) for the new tile with a notched trowel, which you can rent at a tile store or home center. Keep the mastic at least 1/4" from the edge of the new tile to prevent the glue from oozing up between adjacent tiles. Set the new tile in place, positioning its edges tightly against surrounding tiles, and then press down in the center. (*Illustration D.*) If there is any excess mastic, wipe it away immediately. Use heavy weights (i.e., books, bricks, etc.) to hold the new tile in place overnight.

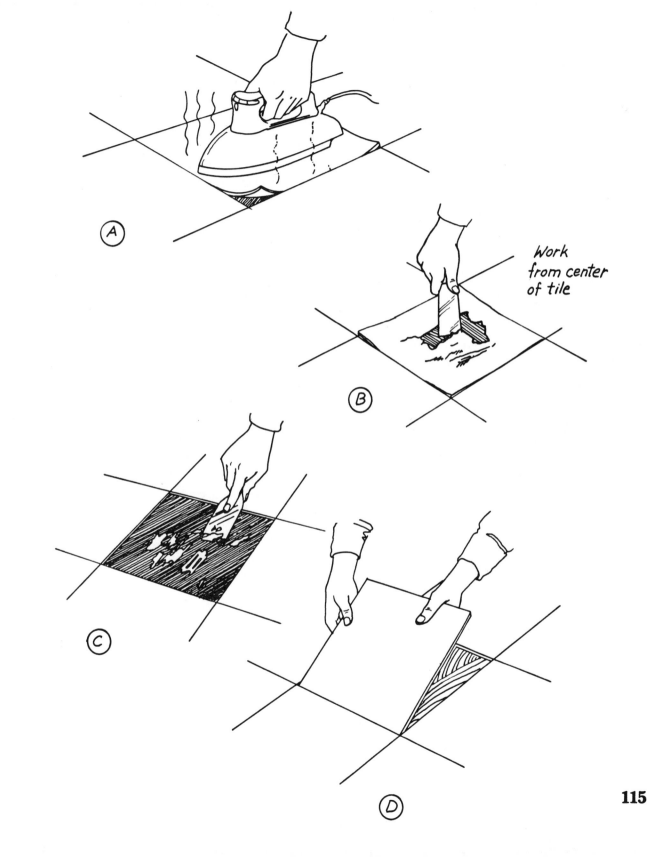

Work from center of tile

A

B

C

D

115

Carpet Repairs

Tools: Scissors or razor blade, steel straight edge or try square, utility knife

If you have a burn or unremovable stain in your carpet, you can make a patch repair by cutting out the bad section and replacing it with a new one.

1) Clip off singed carpet strands of shallow burn

If just the top ends of the carpet fibers are scorched, you can try this remedy. Randomly snip off the ends of the damaged fibers with a sharp pair of scissors (*Illustration A*) or slice them off with a razor blade. Most of the time this will lighten the burned area enough to make it almost undetectable.

2) Locate source of good carpet from hidden area

If the burn or stain is bad, a patch is the only solution. Decide where you can cut a small piece of carpeting to make the patch. One source is a scrap of leftover carpeting. Another idea is to take the patch from an inconspicuous area under a large piece of furniture that is rarely moved or from inside a closet.

3) Cut out bad section of carpeting

Use metal straight edge or a try square to guide your utility knife. (*Illustration B.*) Cut out the damaged spot in a triangular or rectangular shape. (*Illustration C.*) Make sure the blade on the knife is razor sharp to ensure cutting a clean patch.

4) Cut patch to fit hole

Place the bad piece of carpet on the area you have chosen to cut the patch from. Check that the pattern and carpet pile match. If you are using a scrap of leftover carpeting, cut it from the back (underside). In either case, use the bad section as a pattern.

5) Use double-stick tape to hold patch

Lift up the carpet in the area to be patched and place strips of double-stick tape around the edges of the patch hole. (*Illustration D.*) Also stick the tape to the back of the carpet, then press the carpet down to the floor. Put the patch in place, check the match of the pile and pattern, and press it tightly against the double-stick tape. Step on the patch area several times to assure that it is stuck to the carpet tape.

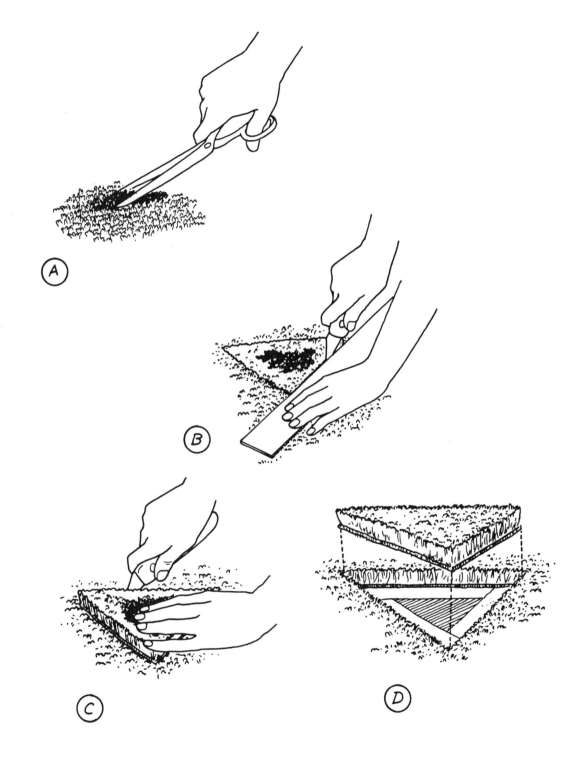

Spot Repairs for Finished Wood Floors

To prevent stains from damaging your floors, keep them well waxed and always wipe up any spilled liquids immediately. But when an accident does happen, here are some "home remedies." Remember, when removing a stain, always begin at the outer edge of the stain and work toward the middle to prevent it from spreading.

Wax or chewing gum

Freeze the wax or gum to harden it by placing a plastic bag filled with ice cubes over it until it becomes brittle. Then scrape away the material with a plastic spatula and recoat the floor with floor polish.

Blood

Use an ammonia solution to sponge or mop away the stain. Combine ammonia and cold clear water (half and half) to make up the solution.

Coffee, fruit juices

Rub the spot gently with a scouring powder and a cloth dampened in hot water.

Alcoholic beverages

First, try a solution of detergent and warm water. If that doesn't remove the stain, try gently rubbing it with a cloth dampened with any of the following: liquid or paste wax, silver polish, ammonia, boiled linseed oil, or denatured alcohol. Afterwards, rewax and polish the floor.

Grease, oil

Remove excess grease or oil with paper towels or newspaper. Then saturate a cloth with dry cleaning fluid and drench the stain, checking it every few minutes.

Mold, mildew

Apply mild cleaning fluid (3/4 water and 1/4 household bleach mixture) to the stain with a soft rag. By providing your wood floors with proper ventilation that eliminates damp, stagnant air, you can prevent this problem from recurring.

White ring from standing water

Rub the stain with No. 1 steel wool and rewax the area. If that doesn't remove the white ring, use a very fine-textured sandpaper and lightly sand the stain. Clean the stain and surrounding area with No. 1 steel wool and mineral spirits or a floor cleaner. Let the floor dry, then apply a matching wood floor finish. Feather (spread thinly) the new finish into the surrounding area and let it dry. Then rewax and polish the floor.

Dark stain or spots

Clean the spots and surrounding area with No. 1 steel wool and a floor cleaner or mineral spirits. Thoroughly wash the area with a rag dampened with household vinegar. Wait a few minutes; hopefully the spots will disappear. If the spots remain, sand them with fine textured sandpaper, feathering out 3–4 inches into the surrounding area. Then rewax and polish the floor.

Very dark stain or spots

If repeated applications of vinegar do not remove spots in your wood floor, apply a solution of oxalic acid prepared to the specifications of the manufacturer's label directions. Oxalic acid, a bleaching agent, is available in hardware and paint stores. Whenever it is used, the treated floor area will have to be stained and refinished to match the original color. According to label directions, let the solution remain on the spots for a while; then sponge them off. Several applications may be necessary for the stains to be removed.

Rejuvenate old wood finish

To repair small areas of wood floors that have been finished with a penetrating sealer, use steel wool to smooth out the affected boards and a few inches of the surrounding area. Then brush on one or more thin coats of the penetrating sealer, feathering it into the old finish to prevent overlap marks. Allow for drying time in between coats. Finally, rewax the repaired area and polish the entire floor.

Spot Removal for Resilient Flooring

The hard finish on today's resilient flooring can be damaged by chemical cleaners. Always try out such chemicals in a small inconspicuous area before using them on a large surface. Here are some cures for stubborn stains, using household remedies you probably have on hand.

Stubborn stains

Black heel marks can be removed with a pen-ink eraser. For other stains, use a cloth dipped in ammonia and water, rubbing alcohol, household white vinegar, or lighter fluid. Rub gently to remove stains.

Chewing gum

Remove as much gum as you can by scraping it up with a dull knife blade or spoon. If the gum is soft, harden it with ice cubes wrapped in a plastic bag. Remove and then use a dab of dry cleaning fluid or paint thinner on a soft rag. If the tiles are rubber, do not use any solvents such as acetone or paint thinners.

Wet paint

If it is a latex paint, wipe away any excess with paper towels. Wash the area with lukewarm water and a mild detergent, repeating when necessary. Rinse with clean water. If it is an oil-based paint, remove any excess with paper towels and use a small amount of paint thinner on a soft rag. Rub gently and repeat when necessary.

Spots in ceramic tile

Ceramic floor tiles have never been more popular than today. The durable floor covering requires a damp mopping with water, plus your favorite detergent for day-to-day care.

To revitalize long-neglected glazed or unglazed ceramic floor tiles, mop a scouring powder paste over the surface and let it stand 5–10 minutes. Then scrub with a nylon scrubbing pad, rinse with clean water, and wipe dry.

For a quarry tile floor, use a scouring powder paste or an all-purpose cleaner, making sure to rinse the floor thoroughly.

Grout stains

The grouting material between tiles can become dirty and discolored. Here are some remedies to remove stains from grout joints:

• *Ink, colored dyes:* Let household bleach stand on the stain until it disappears, making sure to keep the surface wet all the time. Then rinse with water and let dry.

• *Blood:* Dip a cloth or toothbrush in household bleach or hydrogen peroxide and rub into the grout. If the stain persists, repeat the application. Rinse the grout with water and let it dry.

• *Coffee, tea, food, fruit juices, lipstick:* Use a detergent mixed with hot water dipped on a cloth or toothbrush, followed by household bleach. Rinse with water and let dry.

• *Nail polish:* First, dissolve the polish with polish remover. If the stain remains, use household bleach; then rinse with water and let dry.

Spot Cleaning Carpet Stains

Here is a list of common stains and suggested treatment. Remember, the most important thing is to take immediate action before the stain has time to settle into the fibers of the carpeting.

Ink

Use denatured alcohol to blot up ballpoint pen ink.

Paint

For latex paint, treat with warm water after first blotting up excess. Rub gently, going with and then against the carpet's pile. For oil-based or acrylic paint, use a rag dampened with turpentine.

Lipstick

Blot the stain with dry cleaning fluid, followed by a scrubbing with a detergent and vinegar solution (1 teaspoon of each in a quart of warm water). Then rinse the stain with a solution of 1 tablespoon of ammonia in a cup of water.

Wax, grease, tar

Scrape the stain gently with a dull-bladed knife or spoon to remove excess. Treat the stain with dry cleaning fluid on a rag; then rub gently.

Fruit juices, animal stains

If the stain has changed the color of the carpeting, it's likely that it cannot be removed. If the stain is wet or fresh, make repeated sponge applications using lukewarm water after first blotting up excess with paper towels. Apply a detergent solution (1 teaspoon detergent in a quart of warm water), wait 10 minutes, blot again, and rinse the area with clean water. You may have to do this several times to get results.

SECTION 7

Door and Window Repairs

Unstick a Binding Door

Tools: Screwdriver, hammer, wood plane

Through the years all buildings settle (change shape) and interior doors that once worked smoothly might stick. These minor sticking problems can also be caused by a change of season or humidity, but they are not difficult to fix.

1) Mark area where door binds

To fix a sticking door, open and close it several times and note where it binds. Mark the spot with chalk or a pencil. If the binding is not obvious, place a piece of paper between the door and jamb (door frame). Open and close the door as you move the paper around; the paper will stick wherever the door binds against the jamb.

2) Look for loose strike-plate or lock face-plate screws

If the door binds at the strike plate (metal plate opposite the latch bolt into which it fits), tighten the screws that hold the plate against the door frame with a screwdriver. If the screws are loose in the holes, remove them. Dip the end of a wooden matchstick in carpenter's glue and insert it into the screw hole. Break the match off flush with the plate, then replace the screw. Tighten all screws and recheck for binding.

3) Look for loose hinge screws

Look at the hinges. If the hinge screws are loose in either the door or jamb side of the hinge, tighten them with a screwdriver. If a screw turns in its hole but does not tighten, then the hole has become oversized. Repair the oversized hole by removing the screw. Dip the end of a wooden matchstick into carpenter's glue and force it into the hole. Break the match off flush with the hinge and reinstall the screw. Tighten all hinge screws and recheck for binding.

4) Remove door

Remove the door from the jamb if it continues to stick after you have tightened the hinge screws and strike-plate or face-plate screws. First, open the door and place a stack of magazines under it for support. Use a hammer and screwdriver to drive the lower hinge pin up and out. (*Illustrations A and B.*) Then remove the center and top hinge pins. Slide the door off its hinges and place it on a blanket, hinge side down. Slide the blanket and door into the corner of your room so adjoining walls will hold it upright.

5) Shave down high spots on the door

The paint will usually be worn away from the high spots on the door's edge, or use the pencil marks you made in Step #1 above as a guide. Push a wood plane in the direction of the wood grain. (*See lower illustration.*) Make only two or three passes with the plane; then replace the door and check your progress. To prevent the wood from splitting, work the plane from the edges towards the center when removing wood from the top or bottom of a door. Plane away as little wood as possible, since the door will shrink when the humidity drops. When the door works smoothly, apply a similar stain and varnish, or paint the repaired area to match the original door finish.

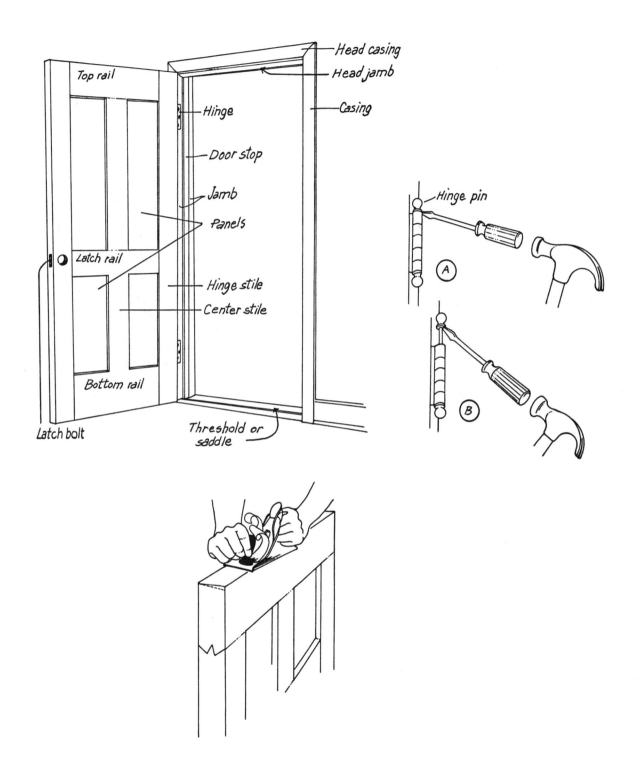

Top rail

Head casing

Head jamb

Hinge

Casing

Door stop

Jamb

Panels

Latch rail

Hinge stile

Center stile

Bottom rail

Latch bolt

Threshold or saddle

Hinge pin

A

B

Fix a Sagging Screen Door

Tools and Materials: Wire brace, T-brackets, turnbuckle, drill, screwdriver

A well-used screen door sometimes sags, gets out of square, or sticks in its frame. These problems are not difficult to cure. However, before proceeding with this repair, first check to see if the door's hinge screws have worked loose. If so, repair the oversized screw holes with matchsticks as described in the repair on page 122.

1) Check swing of door

Open and close the screen door. If it sticks along the bottom or at the top edge of the handle side, it most likely has sagged out of shape. To make sure, lift up on the handle as you close the door. If the sticking is gone, then the problem is that the door sags. If lifting up on the handle does not cure the sticking, then see the repair on pages 122-23.

2) Install diagonal wire brace

A wire brace strung from the bottom corner opposite the hinges to the top corner on the hinge side will pull the door back into shape. Buy a couple of 3″ metal T-brackets, 10 feet of utility wire, and a small turnbuckle.

3) Place T-brackets in opposite corners

Install one T-bracket on the inside face of the door frame in the upper corner on the hinge side. Position the bracket so that the stem of the "T" is facing the opposite corner. Mark the location of the bracket's mounting screws with a pencil. Remove the bracket and drill 1/8″ pilot holes through these marks and screw the bracket in place. Install the other T-bracket in the opposite corner at the door bottom.

4) Cut wire and install turnbuckle

String the wire from bracket to bracket. Cut the wire in the center and install the turnbuckle. Open the door about halfway before you twist the wires tight. Then tighten the turnbuckle until the door is pulled back into shape and does not stick.

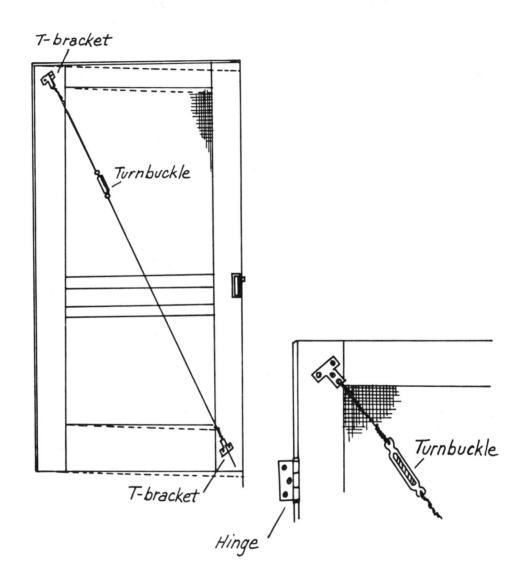

T-bracket

Turnbuckle

T-bracket

Turnbuckle

Hinge

125

Repair Weatherstripping on a Door

Tools: Paint scraper or putty knife, general-purpose scissors, tape measure, screwdriver

Door weatherstripping is designed to prevent cold air leaks in the winter and warm air leaks in the summer. Since it saves money all year long, weatherstripping gives you a quick payback on your investment of materials and time.

Testing door for drafts

If you're not sure if your doors are leaking air, make a simple draft detector by taping a strip of facial tissue to a pencil. On a breezy day, hold your draft detector near the edge of the door and move it slowly along the joint between the door and frame. If the tissue moves, you need to upgrade the weatherstripping. Also check under the door; air leaks at the door's threshold are common.

Weatherstripping a standard door

Weatherstripping is available in various types and sizes and a wide range of prices. One of the most effective and longest-lasting types of weatherstripping is the V-shaped spring-metal type. This style is now available in an easy-to-install, V-shaped, self-sticking plastic version. Measure the length and width of your door and buy a kit designed to weatherstrip your size door. If you have a threshold leak, get an easy-to-install door sweep to stop the air leak between the door bottom and threshold.

Use the illustration on the right as a general guide for how to install the weatherstripping, but follow the manufacturer's directions carefully.

Weatherstripping a sliding door

If you need to weatherstrip a sliding door, purchase a kit designed for that type of door. Use the illustration at the right as a general guide, but follow the manufacturer's instructions carefully.

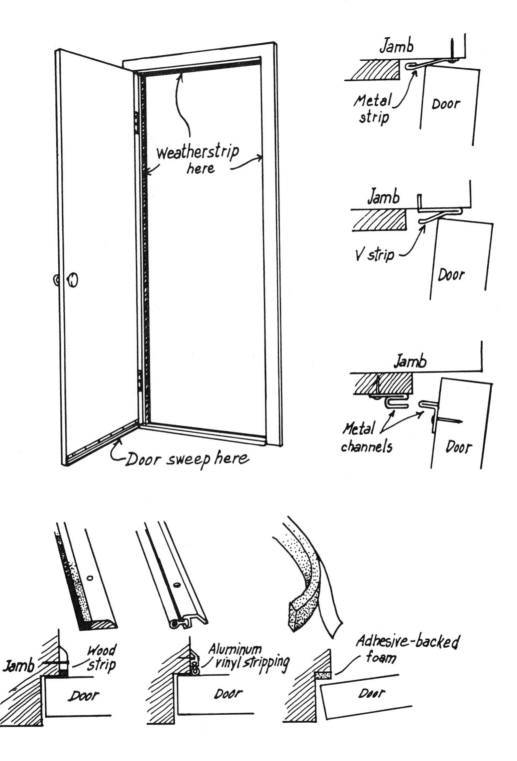

Jamb

Metal strip

Door

Jamb

V strip

Door

Jamb

Metal channels

Door

weatherstrip here

Door sweep here

Jamb

Wood strip

Door

Aluminum vinyl stripping

Door

Adhesive-backed foam

Door

Adjust an Interior Door to Open over Carpeting

Tools: Hammer, screwdriver, crosscut saw, wood plane, C-clamps

New carpeting, especially long-pile types, can make a door difficult, even impossible, to open. The solution is simple enough: just cut or plane the bottom of the door to clear the new carpet.

1) Check door for clearance

Check the clearance between the bottom of the door and the carpet. If the door will not open or it is very difficult to move, you need to remove 1/2" or more of the bottom of the door. This is best done with a saw. However, if the door rubs the carpet but can be opened, you can plane away the excess wood because only 1/8" or less needs to be removed. Mark the bottom of the door with chalk or pencil for a guide when using the plane.

2) Remove door from hinges

Remove the door from the jamb or door frame. (See illustration, page 123.) First, open the door and place a stack of magazines under it for support. Use a hammer and screwdriver to drive the lower hinge pin up and out. (*Illustration A.*) Then remove the center and top hinge pins. Slide the door off its hinges and place it on a set of sawhorses for support, or prop it up as indicated on page 122.

3) Use straight edge to guide saw

Use a saw to remove over 1/8" of wood from the door bottom. With a pencil or piece of chalk, draw your cutting line along the bottom of the door. Clamp or tack a straight piece of wood along this line to guide your saw, then cut the excess wood from the bottom of the door. (*Illustration B.*)

Install the door and test its swing. If more wood needs to be removed from the bottom, go on to Step #4 and plane the bottom of your door to the correct height. When satisfied with the clearance, sand the bottom smooth and apply a coat of varnish or paint to the raw wood.

4) Plane excess wood from door bottom

Use a plane to remove just a little wood (less than 1/8") from the bottom of the door. Work from the sides of the door toward the center to prevent splitting the corners of the door. (*Illustration C.*) Work on one half of the door, then turn it over and complete the other half. When you have planed off enough wood so that the door swings freely over the carpet's pile, sand the bottom smooth and paint or varnish to protect it.

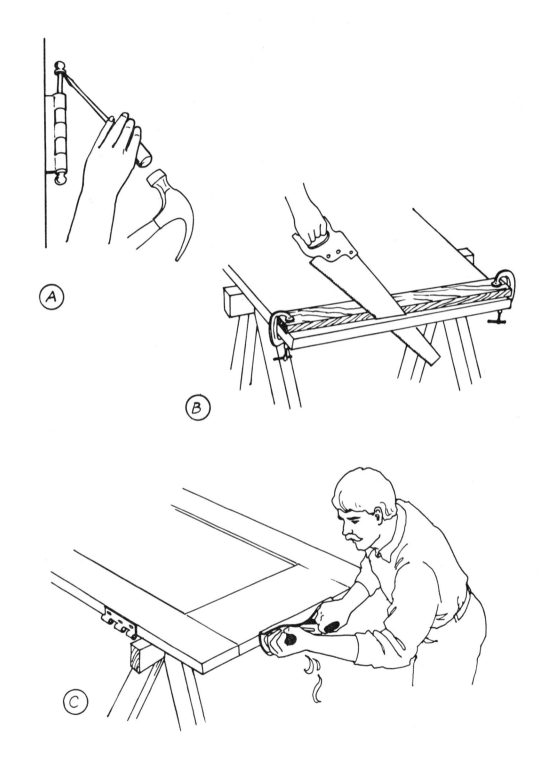

Adjustments to Closet Sliding Doors

Tools: Screwdriver, pliers or adjustable wrench

The sliding doors in your closets are supported by rollers riding in overhead tracks. Many times all that is needed to get these doors back in operation is checking to see that the tracks are free of dirt or an obstruction.

1) Clean track and check for free movement

If your sliding door jumps its track or is difficult to move, check the guides that keep the doors vertical and aligned in the track. Possibly one of the rollers was forced up and out of its track when something got jammed in its way. The easiest solution is to remove the door.

Use a screwdriver to unscrew the floor guide located on the floor at the center of the door or on the wall. Look to see which side the roller is on, and then swing the bottom of the door away from the roller side and lift it up and off its track. (*Illustration A.*)

Use a household cleaner to clean the track. Check to see that the rollers can all turn and are not bent. Reinstall the door and make sure that the rollers can now operate smoothly.

2) Adjust rollers for best door alignment

If the door rubs on the floor or track, adjust the height of the roller assemblies. Some rollers have a bolt that must be turned with pliers (*Illustration B.*); others have set screws to remove. (*Illustration C.*) You will have to loosen the screws or bolts to adjust the door and then retighten them. Lower the end of the door that rubs against the track and raise the end that scrapes the floor.

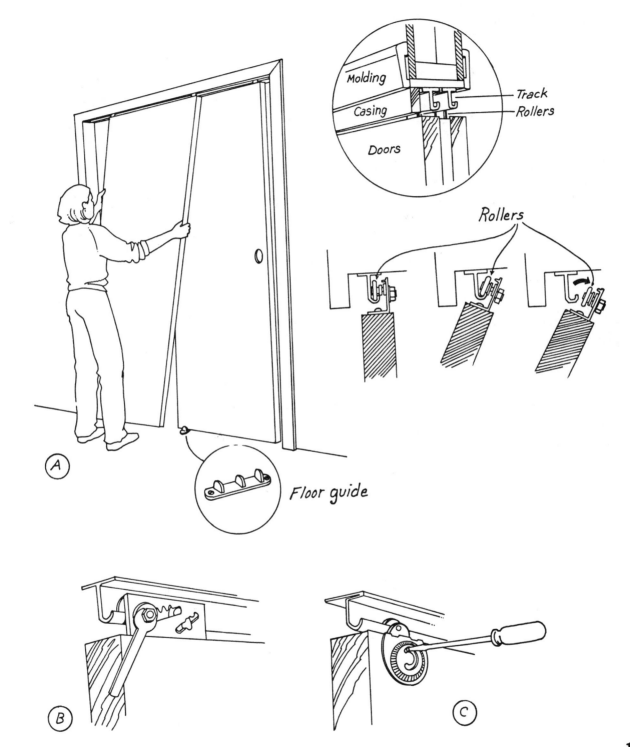

Molding

Casing

Doors

Track

Rollers

Rollers

Floor guide

A

B

C

131

Burglarproof a Sliding Door

Tools: Drill, 1/8" drill bit, screwdriver, hammer

The "sliding" or movable glass panel of your sliding patio door is not as secure as a standard door. Here are three things you can do to make it more burglarproof.

1) Place wood stop in track

Prevent the door from opening by placing a piece of 2"×2" lumber in the track. Cut it to fit snugly between the door and the jamb or door frame. (*Illustration A.*) As long as the wood is in the track, the door cannot slide back to open.

2) Install overhead track screw

If your door can be easily lifted off its track, install 1"-long #14 sheet-metal screws in the overhead track. Open the sliding door and drill a 1/8"-wide pilot hole in the center of the overhead track. Thread the screw in just far enough so the door will slide by the screw head. (*Illustration B.*) When the door is closed, the screw will prevent the door from being lifted far enough to come out of the bottom track.

3) Install sliding door key locks

For additional security and a more professional-looking job, purchase a keyed lock designed especially for sliding glass doors. Install it according to the manufacturer's directions. (*Illustration C.*) You can also make your own lock by drilling a downward-angled hole through the inside door frame and partially through the outer frame. Insert a large #16d nail in the holes to lock the door shut. (*Illustration D.*) If you install a keyed lock, keep the key handy and make sure every member of the family understands how to unlock the door in case of a fire.

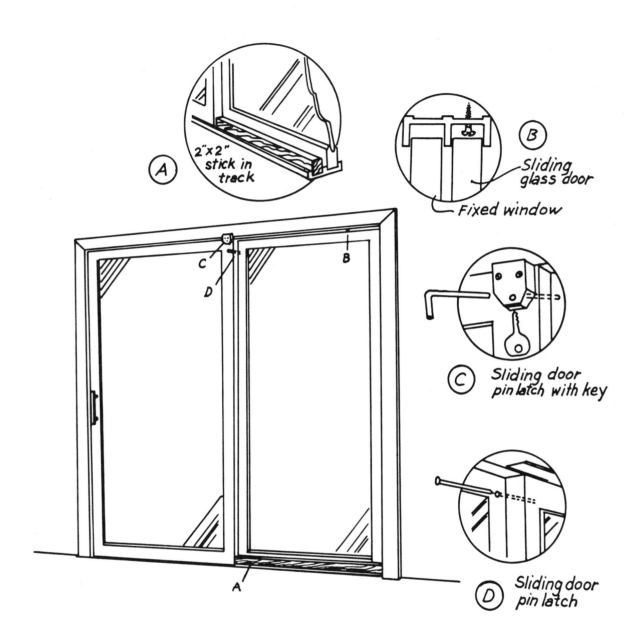

$2'' x 2''$ stick in track

A

B

Sliding glass door

Fixed window

C

Sliding door pin latch with key

D

Sliding door pin latch

133

Troubleshoot Lock Problems

Tools: Pencil, vacuum

Aside from a sticky key, many times lock problems are not caused by the lock but because of a misaligned door. First of all, check that the door is aligned correctly (see Step #1 of repairs on pages 122 and 124). If your door is all right, then the lock is the culprit.

You can solve many lock problems, especially if the locks are the newer tubular and cylinder types. However, if you have an older mortise-type lock (the lock has a long face plate and is set into a slot in the door) and it has more than key problems, call a locksmith.

Sticky lock

If you have trouble inserting your key into the lock, use the crevice tool of your vacuum to suck out any dirt. Rub a lead pencil on the key's teeth (*Illustration A*); then insert it into the lock and work it back and forth.

Sticky latch bolt

By rubbing a pencil's lead on the latch bolt (the part that sticks out of the door edge), you'll keep the latch bolt loose. (*Illustration B.*) Don't use regular oil; it will make the lock work now, but oil will gum up in the future and cause trouble.

Frozen lock

In extremely cold weather, moisture in the air can freeze in the lock. The quickest way to thaw the lock is to insert the key into the lock as far as it will go (but don't force it) and then heat the key with a match. (*Illustration C.*) The key will conduct the heat into the lock.

If you can't insert the key into the lock, use a hair dryer set at "hot" directed at the lock to thaw the ice. Then insert the key and continue heating with the dryer.

If your key turns but nothing happens, either take the lock out (see the repair on page 136) or if it is an old mortise-style lock, call a locksmith for a replacement part or new lock mechanism.

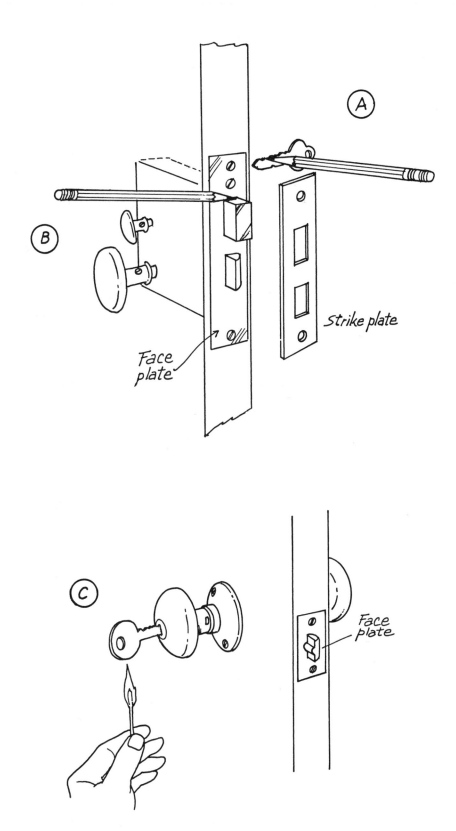

Ⓐ

Strike plate

Ⓑ

Face
plate

Ⓒ

Face
plate

135

Replace Worn Lockset

Tools: Screwdriver

A worn tubular or cylinder lock will feel loose even though all its screws are tight. If opening the door is tricky because you have to work the key up and down or hold it in a particular position before the lock will open, it is time to replace the lock.

1) Remove inside door knob

To remove the inside door knob, push in the button on the shank with a screwdriver. Some types have a small hole in the shaft. To remove the knob, insert a #4d finishing nail into the hole and push; then pull the knob off the shaft.

2) Remove rosette (cover plate)

Remove the cover plate or rosette by inserting the blade of a screwdriver behind it and twisting the handle to snap it off. If the plate has two screws in it, loosen these screws; then remove the cover plate and knobs.

3) Remove lock mechanism

Remove the two screws that were exposed when you took off the cover plate. These hold the lock halves together. Remove these screws and pull the lock mechanism straight out to free it from the latch assembly.

4) Remove latch bolt assembly

Take the old lock to a hardware store and buy a replacement that has the same diameter cylinder (fits into same size hole) and requires the same setback (the distance the cylinder hole is from the door edge). Install the new lock according to the manufacturer's directions, in the reverse order that you removed the old lock.

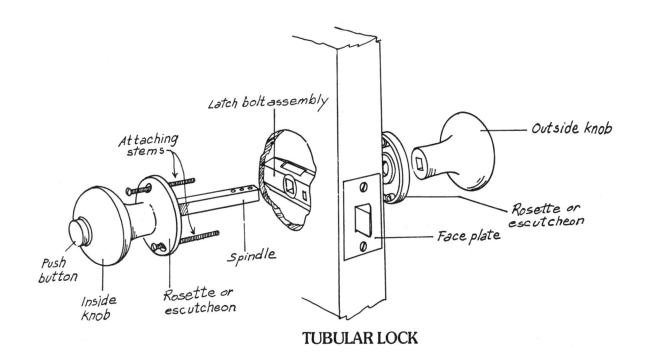

TUBULAR LOCK

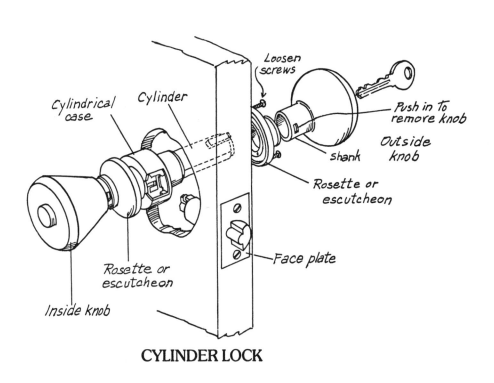

CYLINDER LOCK

137

Fix a Silent Doorbell

Tools: Screwdriver, utility knife

Doorbells are so reliable that it has probably been years since yours was last serviced or repaired. The most likely problem is the doorbell button since it is the only part exposed to the outside weather. But before you take this button apart as described below, check that a fuse is not blown or a circuit breaker is not open in the main electrical panel of your home (see pages 38–39).

1) Remove doorbell button cover

Because the doorbell operates on low voltage (20 volts or less), it's not necessary to turn off your home's main power source. However, be careful not to touch the bare wires of the doorbell or allow them to come in contact with one another until you are ready to test the circuit. Remove the cover plate; it is usually held in place with two screws. Before you attempt to remove the screws, chip out the old paint from the screw slots with a utility knife. If there are no screws, pry off the doorbell button cover by inserting a screwdriver between the cover plate and door frame.

2) Loosen wires and check bell

Loosen the screws that hold the wires to the switch. Hold the wires by the insulation and remove them from the switch. On some button switches you have to remove the doorbell button cover and switch to get at these screws. Touch the wires together. If you hear the bell ring, the button switch is faulty. Take the switch to the hardware store and buy a replacement.

If the bell does not ring, then look carefully at the wires. If you touch them together and see a small spark, then the transformer is good and the problem probably lies in the bell or with a broken or loose wire. If your system has a bell and you have checked out the wiring and switch, and the system still does not work, you can purchase a replacement bell. They aren't expensive and there are only two wires to attach. But remember, there could be other problems in your system; finding these faults can be a tricky detective job requiring a circuit tester. If these simple steps don't get the bell ringing, call an electrician.

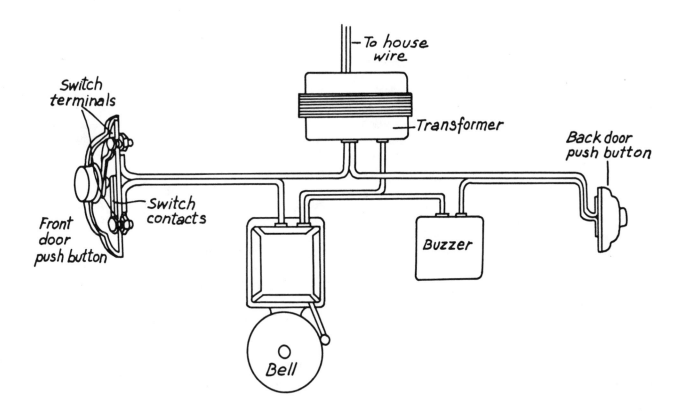

Switch terminals

Switch contacts

Front door push button

To house wire

Transformer

Back door push button

Buzzer

Bell

Unstick a Window

Tools: Hammer, putty knife, wedge or pry bar, chisel

If your windows won't budge, chances are that they were painted shut by the previous owner. While this condition might cut down on a draft in the winter, it is a real inconvenience in the summer. But if the frames are not layered with many coats of paint, the problem could be caused by a change in humidity causing the frame and window to swell and stick. In either case, unsticking a window can be frustrating. Here are a few basic steps to remedy the situation.

1) Open joints with putty knife

Use a hammer to drive a wide putty knife between the window sash and stops. (*Illustration A.*) Do this on all inside and outside joints, when possible. Tap the end of the putty knife gently with the hammer, being careful of the glass.

2) Pry window open

If the window does not open, insert a wedge, hatchet blade or end of a pry bar between the outside sill and the window sash. (*Illustration B.*) Pry up the window carefully; do not use too much pressure or you will distort the window sash and break the glass. Apply the most pressure to the outsides of the window where the force will be applied directly to the vertical parts of the window sash.

3) Clean tracks

After you get the window to move, use a chisel to remove all dirt and dried paint buildup from the tracks. (*Illustration C.*) If the window has many coats of paint you might have to remove the stops (the strips of wood nailed to the side of the window frame used to hold the window in place) from the frame and remove the window so you can get at the track and window more easily.

4) Sand all tracks and rails

Sand the edges of the stops to remove the excess paint before priming and painting. Allow the paint to set for about an hour; then move the window. Come back in a couple of hours and move it again so it will not stick shut.

5) Apply candle wax to lubricate track

After you have opened the window, rub candle wax on the track to act as a lubricant, to ease its movement. (*Illustration D.*)

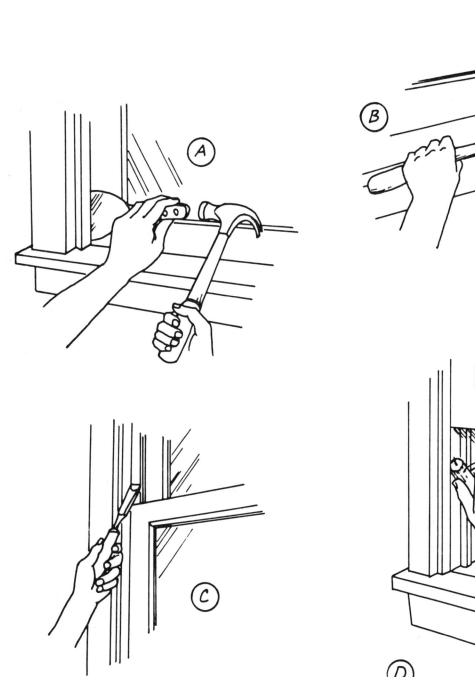

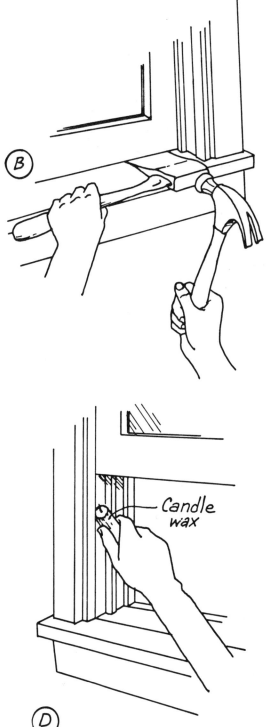

Candle wax

Replace a Broken Pane of Glass

Tools: Pliers, chisel, hammer, paint scraper, putty knife, tape measure

Replacing a broken pane of glass is not difficult. If you have a large storm window or door panel that needs replacing, check with your local hardware store. Their charge to replace the glass in a window or door—that you can carry to the store—is very reasonable. Always replace broken door panels with shatterproof plastic.

1) Remove broken glass

Wear work gloves and a pair of safety goggles to protect yourself as you carefully remove the broken glass from the sash, the window frame in which the glass is set. (*Illustration A.*) Grip the small pieces with pliers and work them loose. You may also need to chisel out some of the old hard putty to remove all of the glass.

2) Remove all old putty and glazier points

Remove the remaining putty with a scraper. If the putty is hardened and won't budge, use a chisel and hammer. (*Illustration B.*) Remove all the metal "glazier points" in the sash with pliers; use a paint scraper on the wood to scrape it clean; then sand it smooth.

3) Seal raw wood; purchase new pane

Paint the edges of the frame with a wood sealer or exterior paint (thinned with mineral spirits) to coat the grooves. (*Illustration C.*) This prevents the wood from absorbing oils from the new glazing compound (putty).

With a tape measure, determine the height and width of the area where the glass will fit. Make a cardboard pattern of any odd-shaped openings and bring it with you to the hardware store when you order the glass or plastic.

4) Apply layer of putty

Spread a thin, even layer of glazing compound around the frame (*Illustration D*), and set the new pane in place. The putty will ooze out around the edges, making them moistureproof.

5) Press in glazier points

Press the glass into position and gently tap new metal glazier points in place around the parameter with the hammer. Space them 4–6″ apart. (*Illustration E.*)

6) Apply putty and smooth with knife

Spread a second layer of glazing compound rolled into a ropelike strand. Use your fingers to press it in place, covering the groove along the edges of glass and the glazier points. Drag a putty knife held at an angle across the length of putty to remove the excess and create a smooth surface. (*Illustration F.*) If the putty sticks to the putty knife, dip the putty knife blade into mineral spirits. This will melt off the stuck putty and prevent further sticking. Wait until the next day to repaint the area.

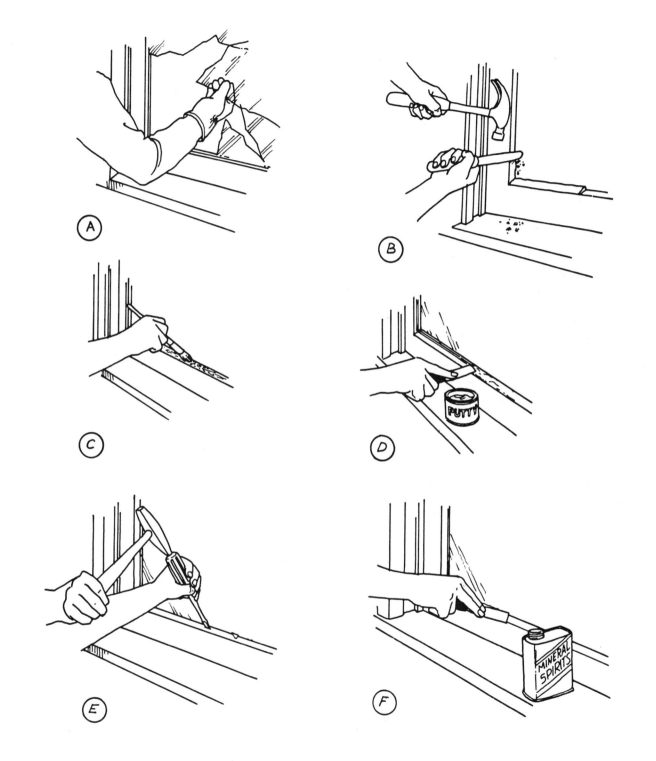

Repair Weatherstripping on a Window

Tools: Scraper or putty knife, large scissors, tape measure, screwdriver

Windows, like doors, can be a source of air leaks. To test your windows, use the same draft detector as described on page 126. Each small window leak adds up to a major source of heat loss or gain because there are so many openings in a house. Weatherstripping a window is a little more involved than weatherstripping a door, but your effort will be repaid with substantial energy savings.

Weatherstripping a double-hung window

As with door weatherstripping, the best-looking and longest-lasting type of window weatherstripping is the V-shaped spring-metal type. This style is now available in an easy-to-install, V-shaped, self-sticking plastic version and is best for double-hung windows (top and bottom sections move up and down).

Use the illustration at the right to see where to install the weatherstripping. Make sure that all surfaces to which the weatherstripping will stick are clean and dry. Follow installation directions carefully.

Weatherstripping a casement window

A casement window is easy to weatherstrip because you can do all parts of the frame at the same time. Use V-shaped, self-sticking plastic weatherstripping. Follow the illustration at the right as to where to place the weatherstripping. Be sure you install the weatherstripping with the point of the V facing toward the outside of the window.

Weatherstripping a sliding window

Sliding windows are not difficult to weatherstrip. The V-shaped type of weatherstripping is effective on the vertical surfaces of the frame. Use self-sticking, tubular, vinyl-type weatherstripping on all horizontal joints. Use the illustration at the right as a guide and follow the installation instructions.

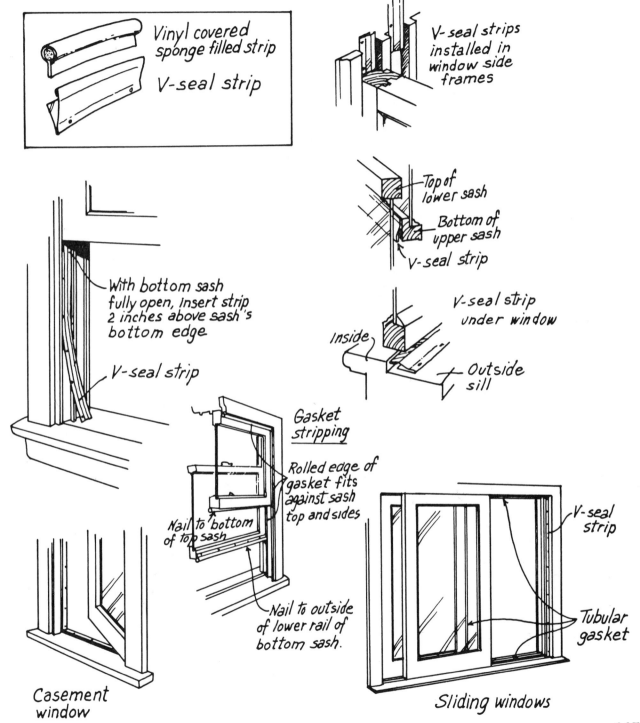

Vinyl covered sponge filled strip

V-seal strip

V-seal strips installed in window side frames

Top of lower sash

Bottom of upper sash

V-seal strip

With bottom sash fully open, insert strip 2 inches above sash's bottom edge

V-seal strip

V-seal strip under window

Inside

Outside sill

Gasket stripping

Rolled edge of gasket fits against sash top and sides

Nail to bottom of top sash

Nail to outside of lower rail of bottom sash.

Casement window

V-seal strip

Tubular gasket

Sliding windows

145

Burglarproof a Window

Tools: Drill, hammer, tape measure, screwdriver, hand saw

Several easy-to-make locks can be added to your windows to prevent them from being opened. If you do install any of these locks, make sure everyone in the family, including the children, understands how to open the window in an emergency.

1) Lock double-hung window with large nail

Drill a 1/8"-diameter hole through the upper corner of the inside window frame and partway through the outer frame. Angle the hole downward slightly. Insert a #16d nail into the hole to lock the window. (*Illustration A.*)

2) Place stick in sliding window track

With a tape measure, determine the distance from the movable window to the opposite side of the window frame. Use a hand saw to cut a stick (a 3/4" × 1½" pine stick will do) to this measurement. To lock the window, drop the stick into the window track. (*Illustration B.*)

3) Purchase ready-to-install keyed lock

On the opposite page (*Illustration C*) are just two of the many types of window locks you can purchase at your local hardware store or home center. These are key-operated and can be installed with a screwdriver and drill.

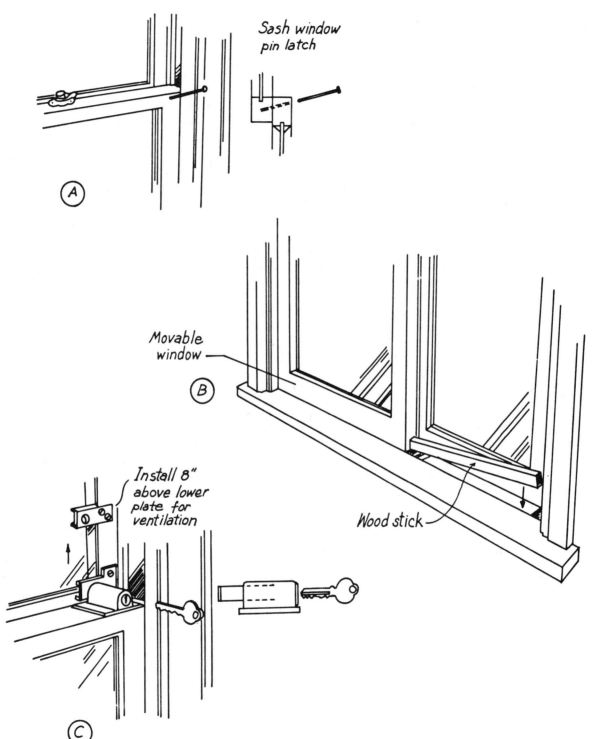

Sash window
pin latch

A

Movable
window

B

Wood stick

Install 8"
above lower
plate for
ventilation

C

147

Repair a Wood-framed Screen

Tools: Stiff putty knife or chisel, 2 C-clamps, utility knife, staple gun, tape measure, hammer, nail set

Window screens are made with either wood or metal frames and their repair is an easy and gratifying job. For both types of window, we suggest using fiberglass or plastic screening mesh instead of aluminum, which is more difficult to work.

1) Remove molding and old screen

Lay the screen on a flat, clean working surface. Place it molding side up, with the thin bead molding facing you. Carefully pry the molding off with a putty knife or chisel. (*Illustration A.*) If the screen is old and in disrepair, take care not to gouge or split the molding so you can reuse it. If the screen is damaged or missing, use a tape measure to measure the length needed and get replacement beading at a lumberyard or home center. (If you plan to paint the screen frame as well as mend it, do so before replacing the screening. It is easier to paint without the screening.)

With the molding removed you'll see how the old screening was tacked, nailed or stapled into the rabbet, or recess, of the frame. Dust off any dirt and remove all nails, tacks or staples to prepare a clean surface where you'll attach the new screening.

2) Cut screen to fit and stretch in place

The most important factor in installing the screen is to get it tight. The easiest way to do this is to bow the window or door. For a screen door, place several boards on a sawhorse and use C-clamps to attach the door to the boards. Place a piece of 3/4"-thick wood under each end of the window or door before you tighten the clamps. (*Illustration B.*) As you tighten them the center is bent, causing the ends to bow up and come closer together, making the door or window slightly shorter.

With a utility knife, cut the new piece of screening several inches larger on all sides than needed. Begin at the top of the frame and staple the screen in place. Then pull the screen tight and staple it to the other end. The screen should be tight enough to stretch from end to end. Next, unclamp the frame and staple the screen to the sides of the frame.

3) Replace screen molding

Using a nail set, hammer nails in to replace the old molding. (*Illustration C.*) Buy new molding if it is cracked or split. Use rustproof aluminum or galvanized brads to hold the screen in place. With a utility knife, trim off any excess screening that sticks out past the molding.

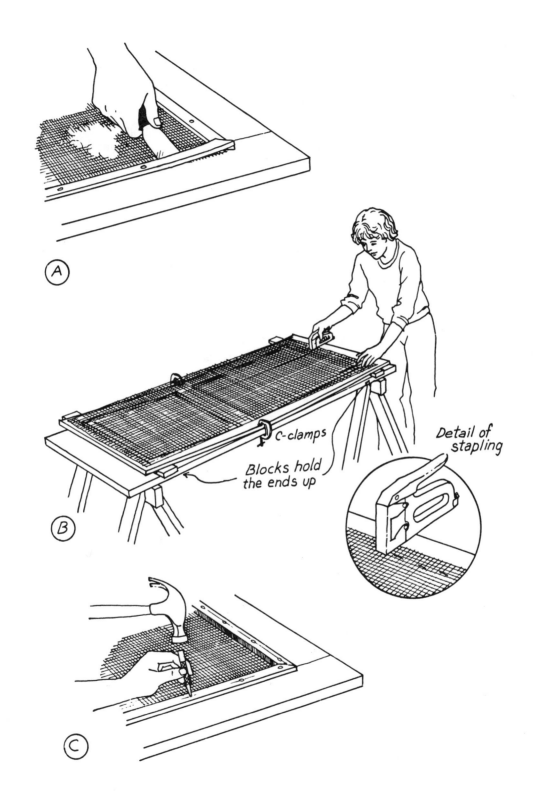

(A)

(B) C-clamps

Blocks hold
the ends up

Detail of
stapling

(C)

149

Repair a Metal-framed Screen

Tools: Try square, utility knife, screen roller or spliner

In a metal frame the screen is held in place with a gasket-like spline made of plastic or rubber. It wedges the edges of the screening in place so there are no staples or molding. This is an easy repair; use a fiberglass screen and purchase an inexpensive tool called a screen spliner or roller (it looks like a pastry cutter).

1) Remove spline to release old screen

Remove the old screening by pulling the entire length of spline from its groove in the frame.

2) Cut screen oversize

Place the frame on a sturdy, clean work surface. Check to see that the frame is square with a try square. Place the square inside the screen frame (*Illustration A*) and if the two don't align, push the frame back into align-ment with the square. With a utility knife, cut the replace-ment screening several inches larger than needed, using the frame as a pattern.

3) Install new screen with spline tool

Place the screening over the frame, aligning it evenly around all sides. Then beginning at a corner, start work-ing the spline into the groove with the spline roller. (*Illustration B.*) Work down the longest side first. Force the splining material into the groove using the roller and con-tinue rolling out the new spline halfway around the frame. Pull the screen tight as you work up the other long side. Pull the screening taut with one hand and push the spline roller ahead with the other. (*Illustration C.*) Cut away excess screening with the utility knife.

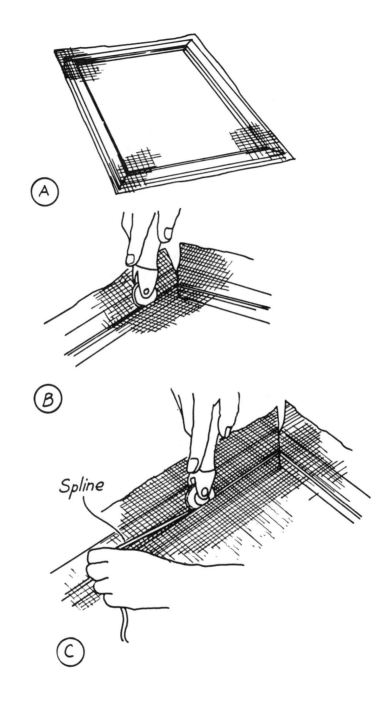

Spline

Patch a Screen

Tools: Scissors

If a screen has a small hole or tear, the repair is as easy as weaving. You can purchase a readymade patch kit at most hardware and home centers or you can make your own patches from screen scraps.

Readymade patch

Lay the ready-cut patch over the tear and weave its curved ends into the screening. Then bend the strands flat to lock them in place. (*Illustration A.*)

Make your own patch from scrap

You can make your own patch by cutting a square piece of screening about twice the size of the hole and partially unraveling half the screen strands from an inch on each side. Then bend the loose strands at a right angle. Thread the loose strands through the screen (*Illustration B*) and pull the patch tight against the hole; then bend the strands flat on the other side of the screen to lock the patch in place. Use scissors to trim the strands if they are long or unsightly.

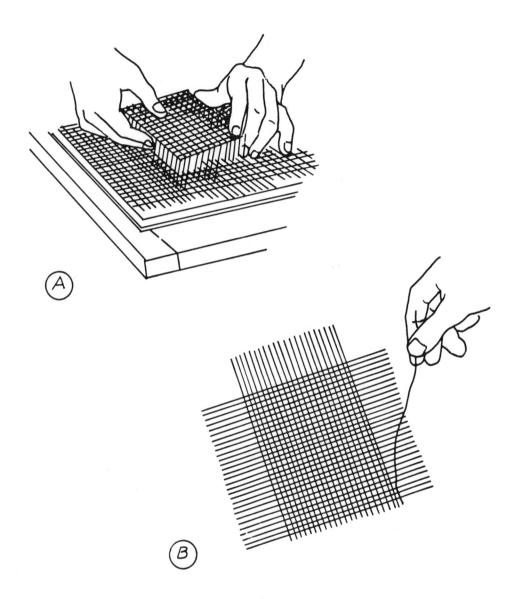

Repair a Window Shade

Tools: Hammer, screwdriver, pliers, staple gun

A temperamental window shade can be a nuisance, and more than likely, all that's needed to fix it is a bit of adjustment or minor repair.

Window shades have metal pins that stick out from each end. At one end is a round pin; on the other end is a flat pin that is attached to the retracting mechanism. Behind the metal cap at the flat pin end of the roller is a small pawl that catches in a notch on the flat pin shaft. The pawl holds the shade in position.

1) Adjust mounting brackets for easy movement

If the shade won't turn freely, check the mounting brackets. If the nails or screws that hold these brackets in place are loose, tighten them with a hammer or screwdriver. Check to see that the brackets are not bent.

If the shade is loose in the brackets and one end keeps falling out, bend the brackets so that they are closer together. If the brackets are mounted inside a window frame, use a pliers to pull the round pin farther from the shade body. If this does not work, remove one bracket and put a cardboard shim (wedge to fill out space) behind it. This will move the brackets closer together.

2) Adjust spring tension

If the tension of the shade spring is too weak to roll the shade all the way up, pull the shade halfway down and let the ratchet pawl catch. Remove the shade from the brackets and roll it all the way up. Put it back in its brackets and pull it down. You should feel more spring tension and the shade should roll up.

If the tension is too strong, and every time you roll up the shade it gets out of control, reverse the procedure. Roll the shade up, then remove it and unroll 6 inches or so of the shade to loosen its spring; then reinstall the shade and try the spring action.

3) Clean ratchet pawl

Sometimes a shade will not stay down, or it takes many tries of pulling it up and down to get the shade to stay in the position you want it. This condition is usually caused by dirt buildup in the ratchet mechanism. In the flat blade end of the roller, dirt sometimes collects and jams the pawl that catches in the ratchet teeth. Sometimes the ratchet is located behind the metal end cap; just pull the ratchet pawl off with a pliers. Blow out the dirt; then use a lightweight oil to lubricate the mechanism.

4) Replace roller, if necessary

If you've tried all the above suggestions and your window shade still does not operate properly, you can replace the roller with a new one. Take it to a hardware or specialty shade store to get an exact duplicate. Remove the shade by detaching the staples. Use a staple gun to reattach the shade to the new roller.

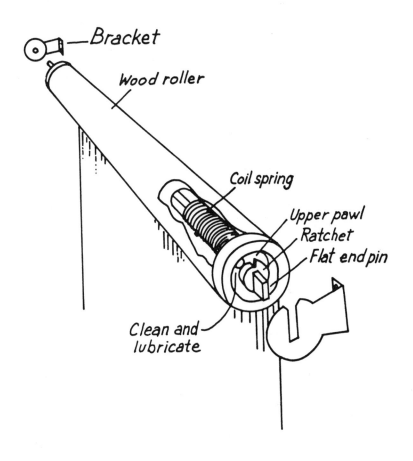

Bracket

Wood roller

Coil spring

Upper pawl
Ratchet
Flat end pin

Clean and
lubricate

SECTION 8

Outside Repairs

Kinds of Caulk to Seal Cracks

Tools: Caulking gun

Caulk is a flexible sealant designed to fill cracks and gaps in all the joints of your house. Caulk ages and eventually dries out, especially around walls, windows, and doors having a southern exposure. When this occurs, air and water can enter your house through these cracks. The most important areas that you should caulk around the exterior of your house are shown on the facing page. Inside your home, check the tub area and recaulk the joint around the tub.

Caulk purchased in a disposable tube and applied with a caulking gun (see page 161) is most economical. There are many types available and each has its own features. Some types are more expensive than others. Generally, the expensive caulks will have a longer life and they are the best buy.

Here are the different types of caulks you can find at your local hardware store. One tube will fill about 25 feet of a 1/4"-wide crack or seal two small windows.

Oil-base Inexpensive; short life; can be painted.

Latex-base Average priced; medium life; can be painted.

Rope caulk Average priced; short life; cannot be painted; only used for weatherstripping and temporary repair.

Butyl rubber Expensive; long life; can be painted; suitable for sealing joints between masonry (stone, brick) and metal.

Foam Expensive; long life; can be painted; suitable for sealing areas too wide for conventional caulk.

Polysulfide Expensive; long life; sticks to painted surfaces and can be painted.

Silicone Most expensive; very long life; cannot be painted.

Important Areas Where Caulk Should Be Applied

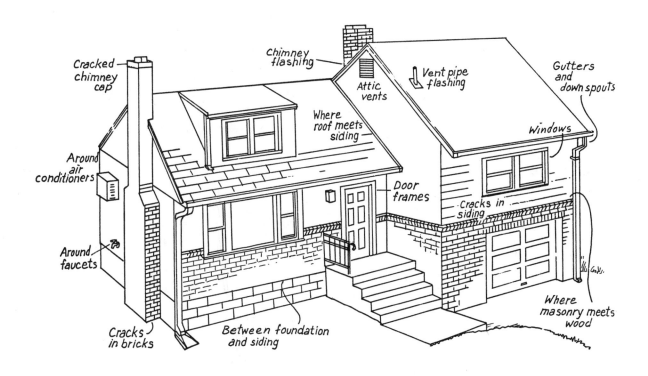

Cracked chimney cap

Chimney flashing

Vent pipe flashing

Gutters and downspouts

Attic vents

Where roof meets siding

Windows

Around air conditioners

Door frames

Cracks in siding

Around faucets

Cracks in bricks

Between foundation and siding

Where masonry meets wood

How to Apply Caulk

Tools: Scraper or chisel, screwdriver, utility knife or scissors, caulking gun

Caulk is sold in cartridges that fit into an easy-to-use half-barrel caulking gun. Check the label on the caulk to see what type of solvent is needed for cleanup.

1) Clean old caulk from joint

Clean the joint or crack that you want to fill by removing all old caulk with a scraper or chisel. (*Illustration A.*) Clean away all dirt with an old paintbrush and wipe the joint with a damp rag. Allow the joint to dry before caulking.

2) Pack oakum into deep crevices

If the crack or joint you have to caulk is more than 1/2" deep, purchase a package of oakum packing, available at most hardware stores and home centers. Oakum is a treated hemp rope that you can unravel to make a strand of desired diameter to fit into a large, deep crack. Place the oakum on the crack and push it tightly into the void with your scraper or screwdriver. (*Illustration B.*) Filling a large crack with oakum is cheaper than using caulk.

3) Cut caulk tube's nozzle, then break cartridge seal

Use a utility knife or scissors to cut off the tip of the caulk's cartridge at a 45-degree angle. (*Illustration C.*) The nozzle is usually marked with several lines showing different bead lines (the size of the cartridge hole). Cut the nozzle at the first marking or make a 1/8" opening in the tip of the nozzle. Push a piece of wire (an old coat hanger) through the nozzle hole into the tube to break the seal.

4) Load caulking gun

Pull the L-shaped caulking gun handle all the way back; then insert the cartridge in the gun so that the cartridge nozzle faces opposite the handle. (*Illustration D.*) Turn the caulking gun's handle so that the notches in the plunger face down. Pull the trigger until you feel resistance.

5) Position nozzle in crack and squeeze trigger

Place the nozzle of the caulk cartridge in the crack you want to fill and squeeze the trigger of the caulking gun while pushing the tube away from you to fill the gap with caulk. (*Illustration E.*) When you reach the end of the crack or joint, turn the handle of the caulking gun so that the notches on the plunger face up in order to release pressure in the caulk tube and to stop the caulk.

6) Drag finger over joint to smooth caulk

As you lay in a long bead of caulk, complete a section at a time and then run your index finger over it to straighten out any misdirected compound. Wet your finger with water if you are using latex caulk; use mineral spirits if you are using another type.

7) Place nail in tube end to save unused caulk

Clean up the area immediately and put a nail in the tube nozzle to save for reuse. (*Illustration F.*)

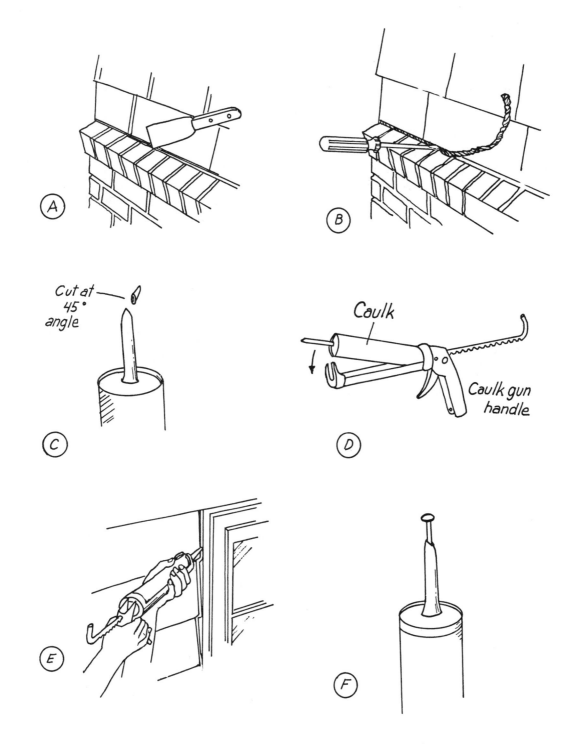

A

B

Cut at 45° angle

C

Caulk

Caulk gun handle

D

E

F

Fix Leaky Gutters

Tools and Materials: Ladder, caulking gun, caulk, wire brush, scraper, hammer, drill, 1/4″ drill bit

Gutters are the troughs hung along the edge of the roof that protect the exterior of your house from water damage. They collect water runoff from the roof and duct it away from the house, preventing it from getting behind your house's siding and trim. Gutters also help keep the perimeter around your home's foundation and your basement dry.

Gutter work is a two-person job because there should be someone on the ground to steady the ladder and to go for tools and materials when needed.

1) Set up ladder safely

Set the ladder base firmly against the wall and walk it upright into position. Lift the base and move it outward into a position away from the wall. Place the ladder base at least one fourth the ladder's height away from the wall. For example, a 10-foot ladder should be at least 3 feet away from the wall. Check to see that the base of the ladder is resting on level ground.

When climbing a ladder, put both hands on the rungs. Don't carry up tools and materials; put them in a bucket with a rope on it and pull the bucket up once you're there. Never lean to either side of the ladder; instead, move the ladder closer to the work area.

2) Inspect your gutters for problems

Four conditions (all repairable) cause gutters to leak: gutters filled with debris; loose joints; a pinhole or holes in the gutter; or sagging gutters caused by a broken support, or "hanger." On the following two pages are ways to remedy this.

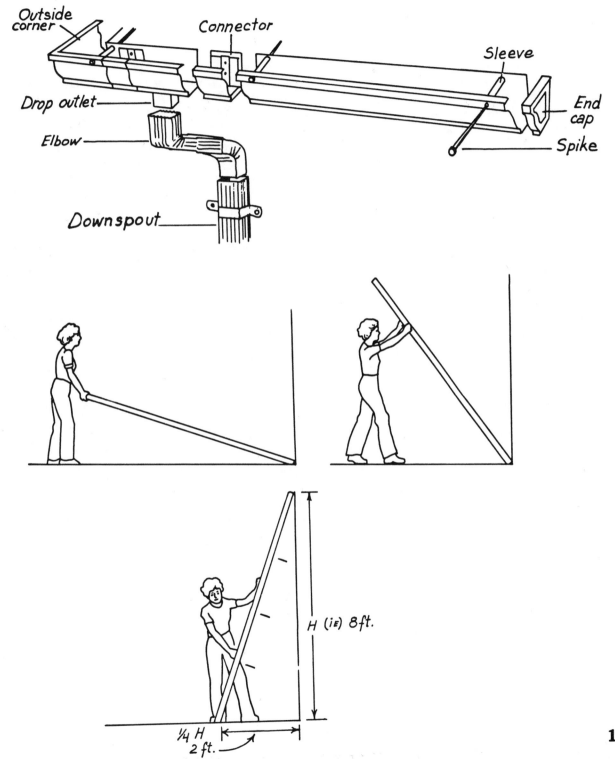

Outside corner

Connector

Sleeve

Drop outlet

End cap

Elbow

Spike

Downspout

H (ie) 8 ft.

¼ H
2 ft.

163

1) Remove debris in and around gutter

Cleaning gutters is an easy but messy job. The fastest method of removing debris from the gutter is with gloved hands. (*Illustration A.*) When most of the debris is out, use a garden hose to flush the gutter clean. Trim tree or shrubbery branches that overhang the house to keep leaves and twigs from accumulating in the gutters.

2) Install anticlog screens and downspout guards

If you live in an area surrounded with trees, purchase easy-to-install plastic or wire mesh screening and fit it over the gutters. (*Illustration B.*) Also insert bird-cage-type guards in downspouts to keep them clog-free. (*Illustration C.*)

3) Caulk leaking joints

Loose joints are corrected by caulking. Use a silicone caulking compound and apply it to the inside of the joint (see pages 160–61). Smooth the caulk around the joint with your finger to prevent it from making a dam that will stop the free flow of water.

4) Use gutter patch to repair holes

Use a wire brush to remove all of the loose or scaling rust from the area around the gutter's hole. Wipe away all dust; then paint with rust-metal primer to prevent rust from spreading. Use a patching compound or roofing cement for small holes. (*Illustration D.*) Choose a cement that contains small fibers to cover the holes. For larger holes, embed fiberglass patching tape into the roofing cement while it is soft. Apply a second coat after the compound sets.

5) Check gutter hanger where sagging is evident

Often gutters sag from the weight of ice and snow. Water collects and spills out at these low spots. Your gutters may be supported by several types of gutter hangers. Sometimes all that is necessary is to bend the gutter hanger back into shape or reattach the hanging strap by hammering in a few aluminum or galvanized nails. (*Illustration E.*)

6) Rehang sagging gutter

The easiest way to rehang a sagging gutter is with a spike and tube type hanger, available at your local hardware or home center store. It is a long aluminum spike with an aluminum tube around it. This type of hanger requires a sound fascia board behind the gutter. If the fascia is damaged, see pages 166–67.

To install a spike hanger, drill a 1/4"-diameter hole in the front gutter lip where you want the hanger. Remove the tube from the spike and place it inside the gutter, directly behind the hole you just drilled. Hammer the spike through the gutter and into the tube. (*Illustration F.*) Lift the gutter into proper alignment and drive the nail through the back of the gutter into the wood fascia. The aluminum tube keeps the gutter from bending.

A

B

C

D

E

Hanging strap

Fascia board

F

165

Fix a Leaky Downspout

Tools: Screwdriver, drill, 1/8″ drill bit, hacksaw

Since your gutters collect the water runoff from the roof and direct it to the downspout, a leak in the downspout can be a disaster. A downspout leak will damage the fascia (horizontal trim attached to the ends of rafters), siding, and foundation of your house. Be sure to set up your ladder carefully before beginning this repair.

1) Check downspout joints and gutter spout

Inspect the downspout where it is attached to the gutter. Its top is usually held to the drop spout, sticking out of the underside of the gutter with a couple of sheet metal screws or rivets. If this drop spout is rusted and leaking, it should be replaced by a professional. Otherwise, push the end of the downspout up over the drop spout and, with a screwdriver, secure it with a couple of 3/4″ #10 sheet metal screws. Drill 1/8″-diameter pilot holes for these screws if there are not already holes in the drop spout and downspout. Check all other joints and refasten them with sheet metal screws as needed.

2) Check downspout hangers

Inspect all downspout hangers. The most important one is located at the top of the downspout, close to where it turns out toward the gutter. Use galvanized nails or screws to replace any missing or loose fasteners. If there is a missing strap, purchase a new one at a hardware store or home center.

3) Check for split downspouts

Check the downspout itself for splits caused by ice and rusted-through areas that leak. Older houses with galvanized gutters have round downspouts; newer ones have rectangular-shaped aluminum downspouts. If you have a bad section of downspout, replace it. Downspouts are available in curved sections called "elbows" and 10-foot straight sections.

If you have to cut the downspout to length with a hacksaw, measure from the crimped end and cut off the open end. When fitting the pieces together, remember that the open end faces up; the crimped end slips inside to prevent leaks.

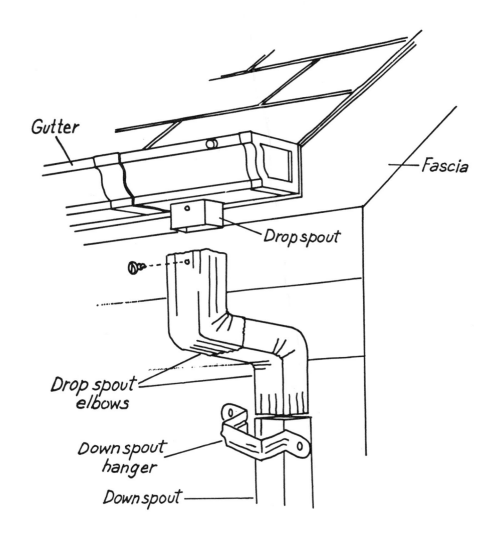

Gutter

Fascia

Drop spout

Drop spout
elbows

Down spout
hanger

Down spout

167